...selling all his life, relishing the pleasure of collecting and the excellent profits that result from years of accumulated experience. He's shifted countless car-loads of stuff at car boot sales, both alone and when helping friends, and developed techniques to snag every potential customer and keep them spending. Every single car boot sale he's been to, as either stallholder or browser, has built his knowledge of the bargaining process, and how to make it work. He's put some of this to good use by writing on collecting and investing in automobilia for *Octane* magazine; some of his 30-plus books include *Chapman's Car Compendium* and *My Dad Had One of Those*, and elsewhere he has won awards for his consumer journalism. He lives in Kent...and owns an estate car.

How To Make Money At Car Boot Sales

Giles Chapman

ROBINSON

ROBINSON

First published in Great Britain in 2015 by Robinson

Copyright © Giles Chapman, 2015

The moral right of the author has been asserted.

A CIP catalogue record for this book
is available from the British Library.

ISBN 978-0-71602-399-9 (paperback)
ISBN: 978-0-71602-400-2 (ebook)

Typeset in Great Britain by SX Composing DTP, Rayleigh, Essex
Printed and bound in Great Britain by CPI Group (UK) Ltd., Croydon, CR0 4YY

Robinson
is an imprint of
Constable & Robinson Ltd

ACKNOWLEDGEMENTS

There are a few people who need, and well deserve, my grateful thanks for their help in the process that has seen this book transfer from idea to reality. I owe an enormous debt of gratitude to Kerry Ball, who gave her time so generously to provide an inside track on car boot sales from a female perspective. I have quoted her throughout the book and have a huge amount of respect for her selling skills. I'm grateful to Nikki Read and Giles Lewis for having faith in the project, but especially to my old friend Martin Gurdon, without whose introduction it would certainly not have got off the ground. Kerry Auger at the Trading Standards Institute was extremely helpful with hard information, and I really appreciate the help of Murray Evans at Kent County Council for connecting us. Another old friend, Dell Stanford, as ever proved supremely resourceful, and I very much appreciate the permission given by fellow journalist Fern Arfin to quote her words. My car-booting friend Anthony Desbrousses must get special thanks for the countless early mornings, constant enthusiasm and shared delight in treasure hunting. I must also give my dad Peter Chapman a mention, as he's the one who instilled in me the discipline of looking at things carefully. And finally, my wonderful wife Annabel: always encouraging, always positive, she read the manuscript and offered her usual insight and sage input. Not only that, but, because I'm often at car boot sales, she and my son Spencer spend many a Sunday morning on their own. No idea what they get up to...

Contents

Introduction

Every weekend throughout the summer, and quite a few during the winter too, millions of Britons spend their free time at car boot sales.

The majority come to seek bargains.

They can be shopping for essential items at low prices, to make their personal and/or household budgets go much further. They may be scanning for stuff that's relevant to a part of their lives right now, such as baby clothes or toys, tools or materials, maybe searching for rare records as a weekend DJ. They can be shopping for their own passions and collections, or be dealers and traders. And, of course, they may just be people who like getting up very early and rummaging, taking the dog along for a walk at the same time.

Sellers make up the smaller component of attendees, and they provide the irresistible pull with their wares. They can range from teenagers selling toys and books they've grown out of, to young mums clawing back money on barely worn children's clothes, to adults with a houseful of possessions to dispose of, maybe after having faced the daunting prospect of sorting out a deceased relative's home. There are traders and specialists, and White Van Men using their trusty vehicles for some weekend cash-raising.

Many sellers are simply tackling the problem of household clutter head-on, turning back the tide on years of creeping, suffocating, dust-collecting accumulation to make life more bearable and the home a less oppressive place to be.

WHAT THIS BOOK IS ALL ABOUT

This book if for anyone and everyone who wants to go to a car boot sale, either to make money or to shop. It is chock-full of useful advice to make the experience enjoyable and worthwhile.

Part One is for those who want to sell at car boot sales. It tells you how to examine your motives, how to prepare for the big day, how to go about setting out your shop, how to make the most of your limited selling time, and how to keep yourself and your property safe. It tells you what you can and can't do at a car boot sale, and it fully prepares you for what can be a frantic, if remunerative, few hours grappling with the Great British Buying Public.

But it goes much further than that, and therefore Part Two acts as a guide for buyers. Of course, it is easy to just turn up and wander around at will, 'grazing' on anything that takes your fancy. Indeed, in many ways, what could be more relaxing? But if you're a buyer with a mission, then I have plenty of tips to help you get the most out of your visit. Crucially, I want to help improve your bargaining skills, so that you can haggle with confidence and without causing confrontations. And I have loads of great ideas about every practical aspect of the day itself.

I decided to write this book after countless casual conversations with friends and colleagues over the years about 'doing' a car boot sale. What struck me time and again was that most people had seriously considered selling at such an event; indeed, they freely admitted they had so much stuff clogging up their garages, wardrobes, lofts, spare rooms and limited cupboard space that doing something about it was almost essential in order to maintain household sanity.

IT'S CLEAR-OUT TIME. NOW!

But something was holding them back. They were constrained by a reticence to actually get on with it, often based on anecdotal evidence from others who had tried a car boot but found it intimidating, overwhelming or unrewarding, and declared 'never again'. Yet a further conflicting factor was the genuine feeling that they'd like to turn unwanted stuff into useful cash. And since the recession bit deep in 2008, making everything go further has become increasingly important to all but the most wastefully wealthy. In the 'boom' years we might have tipped anything superfluous to our lives into a skip at the local council dump; now, though, as the cost of living has risen and job security has been eroded, many of us recognise the very real need to claw something back from our surplus.

I've been going to car boot sales for more years than I can remember, often as a dogged buyer but frequently also as a seller, either on my own or with friends. I've been to hundreds and hundreds of them all over the UK; occasionally I've come away disappointed but mostly I've really made them work for me.

This wealth of experience led me to believe that there was a proper need for a 'manual' that could help the newcomer plan every single aspect of car boot selling in advance to achieve a satisfactory outcome. A book all about how to do it properly. And while I was about it, I wanted to share everything I've gleaned about the buying process, and the awe-inspiring opportunities that car boots present to find and bargain for the things you really, really want.

SELLERS AND BUYERS MATTER EQUALLY

At first, trying to reconcile the conflicting interest of sellers and buyers in one book seemed impossible. But once I'd split the two camps – in effect packaging two books into one, and examining many of the same interactive areas from each entirely separate viewpoint (as I have done at the events themselves) – I began to realise that appreciating one actually fed an understanding of the other.

For markets are adversarial. Buyers and sellers have different plans. But the one thing they have in common is that they both want, more than anything else, to strike a deal and do business. They need each other, to fully understand each other; they may sometimes deplore one another, but they should also respect each other.

Reading my advice for both sellers and buyers should leave you with an extremely thorough, all-round perspective on every aspect of 'booty' trading. Success from either direction is all there for the taking, and my aim is to equip you with the ultimate confidence that you really will achieve just what you want on the day.

CHAPTER 1

What is a car boot sale?

Ever been to Stockport? This handsome industrial town just beyond the outer fringes of Manchester has much to recommend it, and has generated its fair share of Great Britons, including pioneering female TV journalist Joan Bakewell and world-famous architect Sir Norman Foster. Perhaps more pertinently, as far as we're concerned with this book, it's also where perma-tanned bargain hunter David Dickinson hails from. Because alongside Stockport's many proud civic boasts is a much lesser-known one: it's the cradle of Britain's car boot sale phenomenon.

For it was here in the early seventies (as to which year, no one seems quite sure, nor does it particularly matter) that a local Catholic priest by the name of Father Harry Clarke introduced this country to the DIY selling bonanza we now know as the 'car boot'.

For a small charge, you could rock up in your car and sell your private possessions directly and informally from the boot of your Ford Cortina or Austin Allegro.

He'd apparently seen a similar event in the USA while on holiday there. Ordinary members of the public turned pop-up shopkeepers as they sold off personal effects from the 'trunks' (the US term for boots) of their cars on a patch of urban waste ground. In a North American context, it was perhaps a natural extension of the 'garage sale', where householders sold their unwanted bits and pieces on their driveways, perhaps for those living in apartments who weren't lucky enough to own hardstanding and a garage as a ready-made sales forum.

Garage sales have never really taken off in the UK. On this crowded island we are notably averse to inviting strangers across the threshold and on to our private property. I have seen one or two, for sure, but it's usually very young children selling off a few toys at the garden gate to raise pocket money while mum and dad keep a watchful, wary eye.

HOW CAR BOOTS GOT STARTED IN BRITAIN

And so car boot sales got off to a hesitant start in the early seventies. This was the era when memories of the austerity following the Second World War remained fresh. The British public was still in the early throes of 'consumerism', and most homes were not crammed with surplus or obsolete stuff. It was the time when a sock with a hole in it would still be darned, kitchenware would be made to last for decades, and a broom would have its handle and head endlessly replaced.

The few unwanted and frequently worn-out items that were disposed of tended to find their way to scout huts and village halls, where kindly volunteers sold them for pennies to go towards projects like re-leading the church roof. No doubt this was where Father Clarke came in with his Stockport boot sale debut. In fact, as a child in the late 1970s, I well remember one of our neighbours as an enthusiastic early stager of a boot fair. He began to hold them in his capacity as mainstay fundraiser for a preserved windmill nearby, and they caused a brief furore in the local paper. But it was all small, local, gentle and very amateur.

Professional organisation, on a bigger scale, started to creep in during the early eighties. This was no doubt helped by the deep recession at the dawn of the decade and the realisation, particularly by owners of small farms, that more income could be gained from renting out pitches on grassy fields once a fortnight than they could ever hope to recoup by growing veg or keeping a milking herd.

'Flea markets' had never been very popular in the UK – unlike in Paris or Barcelona or other European cities and in the US – with the few long-established events that were held in places like London's Notting Hill and Bermondsey tending to be very early morning affairs (sometimes as punishing as 4 a.m.) where antique and jewellery dealers did their shady deals and those not in 'the trade' were given the cold shoulder. In parallel, weekday street markets offering a little bit of everything were in gradual decline as supermarkets slowly encroached into every niche of the food and housewares markets.

So, in addition to the 'boot fairs' and 'boot sales', 'bootys' and, even, 'boots' springing up across the UK in the eighties, there were now also new 'Sunday markets' – usually held in large car parks or other areas of hardstanding – at which, for the first time, traders, food stallholders, antique dealers and members of the general public were all encouraged to sell alongside one another to create a slightly carnival atmosphere. When organisers of more traditional car boots saw this, they too began to let in professional sellers, food vans, sellers of plants and even children's rides and games to lure the family for a 'morning out'.

TURNING THE TABLES

The most recent development sees the car boot sale coming almost full circle back to its roots alongside jumble sales. This is the 'indoor boot sale' which, of course, is a contradiction in terms because all the selling is done from trestle tables laid out inside a building, and the car plays no part apart from carrying the vendor and his or her wares to and from the event. The restrictions on what can and can't be sold here are obvious. Principally, it is whatever you can get on or under your table, and there are tight space restrictions in place. An indoor boot sale might suit some people but it has strictly limited horizons.

A proper car boot sale stall, of course, almost always has a car at its centre. It can be used as mere transport or as a base from which to sell items, and it will probably be your site office, cafeteria, rest area, shelter and, possibly, even your safe for the duration of the event.

I wondered how an outsider to this country would sum up a British car boot fair, which propelled me to have a look at the United Kingdom section of website About.com (http://gouk.about.com). There, Ferne Arfin, a witty

American journalist based in the UK, has written a snappy guide for her US audience.

'If you can't resist a yard sale and hand-lettered "Garage Sale" signs have you slamming on the brakes and turning out of your way in a flash, then you'll love a good car boot sale. In the UK, people rarely set out garage or yard sales in front of their own houses. Instead, they have giant meets where people who have had a clear out, or who need to raise a bit of cash, bring their unwanted goods to sell.

'Some spring up almost spontaneously – to raise money for a school project or a church, perhaps – while others are regularly scheduled events where hundreds of sellers show up. They combine the qualities of flea markets, swap meets and yard sales on steroids. If looking for treasures amid other people's junk is your thing, you will love a day at a good car boot sale.

'Car boot sales are relatively unregulated. Sellers don't charge or collect sales tax and things change hands in a rather informal fashion.'

So there you have it; we could even see bargain-loving American tourists adding a booty to their list of British must-sees along with Buckingham Palace and Shakespeare's birthplace. And very welcome they would be too.

HOW ARE CAR BOOT SALES ORGANISED?

It's a bit of a surprise, bearing in mind the sheer number of car boot sales being held around the UK today, that there is no national framework for what a car boot actually is, where, how and how often it can be staged, and how much it will cost the organiser for the privilege. Rather than have a set of countrywide rules, it's up to local authorities to license car boot sales as they see fit.

Some councils regard them as simply another form of market, and issue licences accordingly. Others won't permit them to be held unless all the proceeds will be going to a charitable cause or local voluntary organisation. It is a very varied picture from county to county, although pretty much every local authority publishes its licensing rules and other stipulations somewhere on its website.

Apart from insisting on being reassured that the organiser has permission to hold the event on a nominated piece of land, councils need to be happy that the car boot sale won't clash with already established markets nearby. They need to be reassured that litter, noise and disturbance won't be unfairly imposed on local residents. Organisers are almost always required to pay fees to the local authority, which go towards the cost of things like rubbish collection, traffic management and environmental protection. All organisers have to take this into account when sizing up the prospects for a new event.

Councils also like plenty of notice, and to have a detailed plan of what the organiser has in mind. He or she will then need to agree to rules that govern, for example, the type of seller who can take part, the classes of goods that can and can't be sold, and how the locals will be placated when it comes to noise, parking and traffic.

Part One
Selling at Car Boot Sales

CHAPTER 2
Why a car boot?

Britain, as a society in which to live and work and enjoy, is at an age and stage that's unique. There is nowhere else like it, and the reasons stretch back hundreds of years. Once largely agricultural with a few centres of craftsmanship, this nation was the first to undergo an industrial revolution, which just happened to coincide with the explosive growth of the world's biggest empire. Military and maritime dominance zoomed ahead as we shipped gargantuan quantities of raw materials back from Britain's pink-coloured outposts on the world map. Meanwhile, to administer all this activity, we came up with the idea of the mass-produced office worker, and created suburbs and public transport systems to get the most from them.

Somehow, the burgeoning population was dissuaded from revolting against the landowners and aristocracy, and instead poured its energies into consuming. This sparked a new cutting-edge era of innovation and regulation, and while our cousins in America might have started to do things bigger and better than us, we managed to get on top of a World War or two thanks to a mix of ingenuity and diplomacy...before rewarding ourselves with a focus on welfare, education and public health. The last seventy-five years or so have seen fluctuating fortunes, but Britain – where home-ownership and home-improvement built on debt is an absolute obsession – punches above its weight in a variety of niche areas, such as entertainment, research and general one-upmanship.

Bear with me.

We have done an awful lot of things before anyone else. The British lifestyle has in the past had a huge number of elements that, sooner or later, became adopted worldwide, and Britain's largest socio-economic group of people – the middle class – has been pushing forward and self-improving for something close to eight generations; some enormous countries in South America and South-East Asia have middle classes whose background is just two generations old.

Well, thanks a bunch for the history lesson, you may well be saying, blah blah, but what on earth has any of this lot got to do with the car boot sale?

The overall upshot is that, as a consequence of all this and notwithstanding the fact that Britain has some very real pockets of deprivation, we all have a huge amount of stuff.

WHERE WE ARE TODAY

We own a massive amount of stuff, as individuals and as family collectives, because we buy it, because we get given it, and because we inherit it. We tend to accumulate because it's comforting, because we're sentimental, and often because we don't like waste and are vehemently opposed to landfill. And many of us line our homes with excess possessions simply because we're lucky enough to have a dwelling that's big enough to hold it all.

But the fact is, most of us own too many things, and there comes a time, sooner or later, when something major has to be done about it. Here are some common factors that can trigger a call to action:

- House move on the cards.

- Inherited or passed-down items from relations.

- Downsizing to somewhere smaller.

- Growing children, meaning unwanted clothes and toys.

- Relocating to another town, maybe another country.

- Special interests and hobbies have lost their appeal, or you can no longer physically do them.

- Too many unworn clothes and shoes, ladies? (Or, for that matter, gentlemen?)

- Rearranging the layout of your home, or giving it a decorative makeover.

- Getting together with a new partner or, perhaps, ditching an old one.

- Clearing a shed or garage, or changing the design of your garden.

The impetus could be all, some or none of these things. And yet:

It could just be that the material clutter of your life is overwhelming you and you've finally decided to do something about it.

Or

You need to raise some cash!

LOOKING AT OTHER WAYS OF TURNING YOUR CLUTTER INTO CASH

I am biased, of course. I love car boot sales and the opportunities they offer. I've sold at dozens and dozens of them. In my long experience they represent the most effective and least complex way to turn unwanted personal and household items into cash, and to pass on goods of value to appreciative new owners.

Once you recognise how to get the best from such events – and this book aims to give you every possible support – I think you'll share my view that they can, with practice, really work for you. First, however, you need to put them into the context of the other methods of disposal that you could choose. Indeed there have never been so many alternatives. Here are some of them, and the pros and cons of each:

Online auction sites, like eBay

For: You can sell items online from the comfort of your home; a bid battle might ensue, bringing you an excellent return; fully searchable so people can easily pinpoint your things; access to a potentially worldwide audience.

Against: Listing can be time-consuming, especially with a large number of items; payable fees and postage costs can wipe out any real returns; packaging and postage takes time and effort; the disparity between your description and the winning bidder's expectation can lead to stressful disputes.

Online free classified sites, like Gumtree and Preloved

For: The ads are free; you can list from home; you have the freedom to dictate terms; your advert will be searchable and viewable from anywhere.

Against: Agreement and co-ordination required over delivery and payment; if you're posting, then there are the time-consuming issues of packing up and sending via the Post Office or a courier; you may not feel happy about strangers coming to your home to collect.

Online 'free-to-a-good-home' sites, such as Freecycle

For: Efficient to dispose of anything which you feel has little monetary value but could be reused; saves a trip to the dump; stops things going to landfill; contact with local groups and networking.

Against: You won't receive any money; people you don't know will need to come to your home.

General household/local auctions

For: Good for selling antique and collectable items because the audience is mostly dedicated; the organisation and selling are left to someone else.

Against: Hefty commission fees payable; your items still might not sell for much; auction houses can be choosy about what they accept.

Local paper free ads/postcards in shop windows
For: Attracts local buyers; zero or negligible fees.

Against: Timewasters; indiscreet.

Charity shops
For: Good causes.

Against: You'll be giving away your things as donations.

The tip
For: Quick, problem solved.

Against: Unethical...and you'll be literally throwing away your possessions.

THE ADVANTAGES OF THE CAR BOOT SALE
Next to these options, a car boot sale has the following advantages:

- Local – they're staged all over the country, so there will be one near you.

- Concentrated – most are only on for a morning, so it will be over and done quickly.

- Active – you're getting on top of your problem and sorting things out.

- Diverse – you get all kinds of customers looking for all kinds of purchases.

- Cash-generative – you come away with your takings in your hand, in notes and coins.

- Informal – you can sell whatever you like (pretty much – see page 40).

- Fun – it's refreshing to be outside and meeting people.

- Ultimate satisfaction – a great feeling that you are spring-cleaning your life, and banishing excess 'baggage'.

In choosing to 'do' a car boot sale you're taking the best route to disposing of a large number of disparate items within a strictly limited window of opportunity. For a short and intense period you have the chance to sell everything you don't want and turn that clutter into ready cash. If you'd really like to get the bulk of your selling done in one fell swoop, they are unbeatable.

IS IT REALLY ME?

There are, however, some downsides to consider. And the most important one, of course, is you.

A car boot sale is, for a short period of time, quite hard work for which you need reasonable reserves of energy and stamina. You need a willingness to face sometimes unpredictable weather while encountering a wide cross-section of the British public, without becoming flustered or unnerved. You should know your temperament (although your partner might also be a useful person to consult, as they might know you even better!), and if you have serious doubts that you will be able to cope with your morning's selling, as well as the setting up and packing away, then clearly you shouldn't rush into it.

The other major factor to weigh up is that there are no guarantees that everything will go exactly as you would wish it to. Choosing to do a car boot sale will not give the most certain of outcomes – i.e. you might not sell everything you hope to, and taking part in this open market means that you'll be competing with a wide spectrum of other people to gain custom.

But this book isn't for people who don't want to do a car boot sale – it's for people who do.

And, as my old grandfather used to remind me, 'Time spent in reconnaissance is seldom wasted.' Before you so much as start selecting what you intend to sell, you should get yourself along to a local car boot and see how it functions. Wander about, observe how the trading is going, have a good look at the interaction between buyers and sellers, notice the level of pressure the sellers are under as they call out prices, consider offers, take money and put purchases into bags. Most sellers, if they have good stuff for sale, will be hectic but prospering, and will probably be enjoying good interaction with their buyers. You'll see super-salespeople in their element and, in contrast, you'll also clock shrinking violets who apparently make no attempt to interest the passing crowds in what they have for sale. If you can picture yourself somewhere in the middle – your pockets slowly filling up with cash and your merchandise steadily reducing in volume – then:

You can definitely do it!

CHAPTER 3
Choosing an event

There are countless car boots taking place around the UK from early spring to the beginning of winter. How do you know which one is right for you?

Logic, of course, dictates that your nearest one would be most convenient. But the nearest in proximity terms may not be the best for what you have to sell. And if you live in any suburban or built-up area then there will likely be a choice of possible options.

CONSIDER THE LOCATION
The location will have a significant bearing on the types of both sellers and buyers who attend.

In a smart neck of the woods, the quality of the goods on offer from the relatively well-off vendors might be of a higher calibre than the fare on offer at a boot adjacent to a sprawling council estate. And the buyers may well have more money to spend per head.

On the other hand, set up shop at a car boot fair in a less well-to-do area and you may find the demand is stronger for more items at a slightly lower price. Or you've got great specimens, quality brands in good condition that would be beyond the budget for many customers if they were new, in which case the demand could be higher. You could be mobbed by people who are happy to take away almost everything you put out. The price-per-item might end up being less but you will shift a bigger proportion of it, meaning a better all-round result.

Think carefully about how *what* you have to sell will appeal to different target audiences.

If you have a lot of collectibles and antiques – perhaps including pictures, china, glass, ornaments, decorative brass and copper, small items of furniture, upmarket or vintage soft furnishings – you might be better off in an area where people are looking for extra items, presents, additions to collections, or finishing touches for their homes or gardens; basically, a more upmarket and affluent bunch. Choose your event accordingly.

However, if your stuff consists mainly of humbler home furnishings, kitchenware, basic goods and tools and materials, the most receptive market will likely be a little poorer, the houses and flats smaller and the need for low-price goodies greater. They will be working people out to put Sunday morning to good use by getting the most from a limited budget.

Clothes and shoes, meanwhile, will create a lot of interest wherever you choose to sell, a rich neighbourhood or a poorer one, just as long as you have plenty of good-quality high-street brands in among your stock.

All of this is something of an inexact method of forecasting success for your enterprise. Things can be counter-intuitive when it comes to buyers. They might be seeking the lower end of the 'quality' spectrum in the cunning hope that less-informed people just happen to be selling treasure of whose value they are ignorant. Or they could be making the pilgrimage from the less salubrious end of town to the leafy 'burbs because they know a car boot in that area will be packed with quality gear.

Alternatively, a smaller-scale boot fair might attract canny buyers who calculate that there will be less competition, with the more ruthless shoppers drawn to the gigantic affairs, where there is simply more to go for. As ever, no one can ever know quite what to expect, so it's pot luck every time. But these alternate views will give you a good starting point when it comes to picking the car boot that suits your needs.

Size does matter
The biggest of the established car boots naturally draw the biggest crowds, with more of every type of punter. The larger the scale, the busier you are likely to be and, if you have plenty of what people are after, then the more frenetic the morning in prospect.

If you're brand new to car boots, and concerned at how you're going to manage, then maybe pick a smaller one for your maiden outing. Anything between 100–250 pitches would be considered fairly small, and participating would be a relatively gentle entrée into this thriving new world.

CAN YOU COPE WITH THE CONDITIONS?

The traditional domain of the car boot is a field. That means your car, your feet and everything you have to sell will be sitting on top of grass that, as the events tend to kick off at dawn, is almost certain to be wet. The quality of this turf varies enormously in its scrubbiness and its cut, so that even on some summer mornings you might have light mud to cope with. In my experience, you're unlikely to be allotted a pitch that's anything close to swampy, but the ground will be open, uneven and as it comes.

More urban car boots, especially those held in school playgrounds, large car parks, marketplaces or show grounds, and other expanses of hardstanding and, sometimes, gravel, provide solid ground on which to park and set up. For a mud- and grass-free selling arena, obviously these are better. You won't get any dirty splashes on or in your car. And, if you're a chronic hay fever sufferer, this might well be a much more comfortable environment in which to spend the morning.

Bear in mind, though, that this is indeed a green and pleasant land with very much more in the way of available grassy fields than unused concrete and tarmac. Any event where it's rock solid underfoot is almost bound to be on a more limited scale – and that might curtail your selling horizons accordingly.

CHAPTER 4

Making plans for the big day

You've decided that a car boot sale is for you and, perhaps, you've identified a specific event to attend. The day is looming at the end of the week. Now the planning starts in earnest.

IT TAKES TWO – IT REALLY DOES

I see plenty of people at car boots who do the whole thing on their own.

But, despite having sold at countless events and flattering myself that I've got the process off to a fine art, working it alone would never be for me. In fact, I can think of few things as stressful – far too much of an energy-sapping struggle.

A car boot pitch needs two people. And there are a number of very sound reasons:

- **Setting up:** it's a two-person task to get up and running as quickly as possible.

- **Selling:** every successful salesperson benefits from an assistant to keep the transactions flowing, help with packing, cope in a sudden rush, and generally be that invaluable second pair of hands.

- **Security:** one pair of eyes always needs to be alert to the stall itself, no matter how distracting the customer in hand turns out to be.

- **'Comfort':** if you're on your own, there can be no nipping off to the loo, no darting to the snack bar, and definitely no looking at other sellers' stuff.

- **Packing up:** believe me, after a hard morning's takings, having double the man- or woman-power to disassemble your display, pack it all up and repack the car is an absolute godsend.

- **Camaraderie:** it's just more of a laugh doing a boot with someone else.

Who's up for it, then?

Many rookie car-booters like to find a friend to share the whole experience with, and, for the reasons above, I think that's a capital idea.

You can either agree to split the car space to host a stall jointly, splitting everything 50:50, or, if the desire isn't equally strong in both parties, you can ask a mate just to come along with you and keep you company – you can bribe them with lunch afterwards, or a returned favour, but you'll be surprised at how many people will willingly do it just to help you out and, perhaps, have a bit of fun in the process. Whenever car boots have come up in conversation among friends, I've been quite surprised at how many say they've never even been to one but wouldn't mind going.

You've probably got several friends who wouldn't mind tagging along as your oppo for the day, both to lend a hand and to see what all the fuss is about. You never know, it might be their first and last experience of doing so, or they might get the bug and ask you to help out on their pitch another time.

But what about partners, spouses and offspring?

Family activity... or not?

In some ways, it might be harder to prevail upon your close relatives, as they could well have other ideas about how they want to spend their Sunday mornings. Not all couples would relish dong this together, and your son or daughter might get a touch narky if you prevail upon them when they really don't fancy it.

The way to get the family interested is to propose that it's a joint venture – that everyone will have some space on the pitch to sell off their unwanted things. Many children seem to love running their own little 'shop' next to mum's or dad's, and it can be quite a fun way to spend family time together, helping one another out when things get busy. And if your older offspring are at all entrepreneurial, having grown up in the eBay era, then perhaps you could encourage them to give you some help and learn about customer service at first-hand.

Husband-and-wife stalls are also quite common sights. They certainly can work well as they often snag 'his'n'hers' browsing couples with a male and female shopping outlook. But it's essential the spirit of the occasion is shared. I've seen countless stalls where the long-married shopkeepers are in conflict. Whether mild sniping, constant bickering, or open marital strife played out in public, it's unedifying and – worst of all – seriously off-putting to customers.

If it's not something you enjoy doing together, with a shared sense of purpose and mutual support, then don't do it. A 'good' selling couple will not only help each other out but will have the opportunity to play good cop/bad cop with tricky customers, helping to support each other's decisions, whether they be to hold out for a better offer or get rid for fast money.

In my time I've seen all kinds of double-acts selling at car boots – including an awful lot of people with clear anger-management issues and/or what looks like an impending separation on the cards. Only the ones who both seek to enjoy the experience come what may will benefit from it, so for pity's sake don't oblige anyone to be on the business side of the counter unless they're definitely up for it. It's quite a hard morning's work, but it is so much more bearable when two people share it.

WHAT DO YOU DRIVE?

There is no way, really, to sell at a car boot sale unless you've got the wheels to get there. Your vehicle will be transport for everything to and from the event, and your headquarters, storeroom, refuge and safe while selling is in progress.

Organisers at car boot sales seem to draw the line at any vehicle that is larger than the largest of panel vans – the kind of thing Asda or DHL uses for home deliveries – although some might allow in the smallest of trucks and lorries. The unspoken rule is that these must ostensibly be private vehicles driven on a non-professional (i.e. non-heavy goods vehicle) licence.

Clearly, that means a Transit-size van or pick-up would be okay, as would a smaller delivery van. A Luton-type van (so-called because they were developed for the hat-making industry around Luton, and provided extra cargo space for these lightweight items item above the driver's cab) would also mostly be acceptable.

And, of course, all kinds of cars are fine.

I've even seen one or two hackney carriage-type London taxis pressed into use – they are very roomy in the back, after all – and on one occasion a motorbike on which the rider had arrived with his wares in an army-style backpack and panniers, strapped to the luggage rack.

Saloon cars are absolutely fine, but any car with a hatchback is clearly going to offer better cargo-loading options. The best cars for car booting are, of course, estates or people-carriers with fold-down or removable seating. With your two front seats occupied by yourself and your companion, it will give over the whole of the rear to sales stock.

If that's not enough room, you can make use of roof rack capacity if you have it.

Most car boot sales are happy to welcome you with a trailer…because they usually benefit by making a small surcharge for it.

When you pay for your pitch you're generally being allotted a piece of ground about the same length as your vehicle, plus a foot or two extra at either side. Typically, that might be £7–12, so if you have a long van or a car-with trailer, you'll be paying some £3–8 extra for the longer sales space.

Whatever type of vehicle you have access to has a direct bearing on what you can take. But you don't need a massive van to do well. You can pack a mountain of things into even a Ford Fiesta, and it it's mostly clothes and shoes you're taking, then such a small car will be easily able to carry enough to keep you busy all morning.

In fact, you really need to be careful what you wish for. I've often seen a couple of guys struggle to keep on top of a tightly packed Luton van's contents of mixed furniture, bric-a-brac, house wares and trade materials; there is just too much to unpack, formulate prices for and keep tabs on, and these guys look very frazzled very quickly. The quantity is simply too big even for two people, and things inevitably get broken and damaged in the scrum, rendering them unsaleable anyway.

If you do decide to boost your carrying capacity, maybe with a trailer or by having access to a van, it's a good idea to use that extra cargo area for a relatively small number of large and/or bulky items; things that can be unloaded and on display quickly.

Big items can often sell remarkably fast at car boots – even seemingly massive dead weights like three-piece suites, large television sets, cupboards, beds and whole units for bathrooms or kitchens. If you can be bothered to take them along and display them well, then they will most likely go because, of course, most of the visitors will have come in their cars and vans, and so are well prepared to lug their spoils home.

But the fact remains that it will always be harder to find a taker for something that isn't immediately portable. The buyers are all on foot when they pass by your stall, and they intend to visit hundreds more stalls after yours. So the main focus at car boots is always on small, portable items; anything that can be put in a bag or a box and carried without a back-breaking amount of effort.

WHAT WILL PROBABLY SELL, AND WHAT MIGHT NOT

The rules on what will and will not sell are anything but hard and fast. The least likely things can be snapped up, 'dead certs' left untouched. While wandering around numerous boot sales, I've overheard people say to each other, 'You'll never guess what I've just sold!' or 'Can you believe it? That woman just bought all of them,' or 'Yeah, that was just about the first thing I sold at seven o'clock.'

Us car booters are amateur sellers. Very few of us can have any clue as to what will sell on the open market and, anyway, the only things that we have are the items we own and want to dispose of. We're not going to a wholesaler to stock up on strong-selling lines for the Sunday morning retail window.

But there's no doubt about it: some things are easier to shift than others, and this I have discovered through a sometimes exhausting process of trial and error over many years.

I've cleared at least two almost fully furnished family houses of their entire contents, and chanced my arm with most of it at a series of boot sales. And then, with my booting pal, we've periodically routed clutter from our own homes and the spent excesses of our various children. So I have generally learnt the hard way.

Here are some real-life tips to do with what you might call 'hard' objects that I've discovered variously to be shifters and stickers:

It flew off the stall

- **China ornaments:** people make a beeline for these, and the smaller they are the faster they sell.

- **Cribs and cots:** as long as they're clean looking and free of breakages, these go quicker than choc ices in a heatwave.

- **Old TVs and hi-fis:** even if they're unfashionably large, they do shift just as long as the prices are low.

- **Small hand tools:** things like screwdrivers, hammers and planes – working men rifle through them and take handfuls.

- **Jars and containers, with lids:** anything in a set or that's really going to sort out a storage problem.

- **Bicycle-related items:** from whole bikes down to spare parts, car boot sales seem to attract cycling fanatics.

- **'Pairs' or even 'trios':** from lampshades to garden urns, and candlesticks to those famous ceramic triple flying ducks you hang in a row on the wall, if items make up a complete, matching set, then customers will want them.

- **Children's shoes:** as long as they're not scuffed, and especially if they're still with their box and are hardly worn, they won't hang around for long.

Couldn't get rid of for love nor money

- Glasses: I've taken an awful lot of drinking glasses to car boots, and anything that isn't in an unchipped, uncracked set of at least four has almost always gone home with me.

- Picture frames: unless they are spectacular-looking or obviously of top quality, the majority of these have proved very hard to pass on.

- Records: if you have some rock'n'roll, dance or punk gems, they'll be deftly picked out by collectors; but if you take several box loads of easy-listening pap of the Max Bygraves/Peters & Lee/Tijuana Brass/James Last variety, then almost all of it will be back at your house by sundown.

- Video tapes: the time for this format is now long gone – they take up car and sales space and they lie largely untouched by punters.

- Books: as the years go by, newish second-hand (as opposed to vintage) books seem to sell less and less well, especially if they're big and weighty tomes. Children's books, though, always sell well.

- Mugs: they have to be exceptionally attractive examples of the coffee-sipper's friend to get any attention at all.

- Plain, cheap or single plates, bowls, saucers, cups and cutlery: in truth, no one wants these domestic orphans unless they were originally from an expensive set.

- Well-used kitchenware: no one is going to want a fat-blackened roasting tin, glass cookware with burnt-on old food, or worn-out pans with loose, rattly handles. This sort of rubbish is for recycling, not reselling.

As I said previously, these are just a few goodies and baddies that I have personal experience of. Don't let anything I've said deter you from taking whatever you feel might be of interest. Remember, however, that your time and effort will be expended in the same amounts whether you take good, saleable items that you know the British public will find tempting or you offer up real junk that is just one step above skip-standard.

But bric-a-brac and household objects are only half the story at any car boot, no matter how much that area might be the one I gravitate to naturally. Experience suggests that clothes, shoes and accessories generally constitute a little over half of the total quantity of items on offer, and that these things are the most carefully sifted and keenly sought. Most of the vendors and the potential buyers are women, no question, and so I sought out a lady with many, many years of hard-won selling experience for her invaluable insight.

I ASKED THE LADY WHO KNOWS

Kerry Ball, who lives and works in Hertfordshire, is a self-confessed car boot sale addict, rich in expertise in every aspect of the event. As for many of us in Britain today, for her, car boot sales serve a dual purpose. Kerry has to juggle the conflicting calls on her family's limited household budget and so, most frequently during the 'season', she is a buyer.

'I go buying with my friend Jo just about every week,' she says. 'She goes one way and I go the other. I "spot" for her and she "spots" for me.

'Jo's looking for brands in children's clothing, like Baby Gap and JoJo Maman Bebe, that she then sells on eBay to pay for her holidays, and she's really, really good at it. I'm on the look-out for clothes for myself and things for my house, because I'm really into home décor and like to change it around regularly.'

However, Kerry's forte is selling. And every year she will attend three car boot sales: one at the start of the year, one in mid-summer, and the last one as the season is drawing to a finish. She says she buys for resale only very occasionally, swiftly running her mental slide rule over an item that, if it's for sale at £1, she can be confident of reselling for £4–5 to give a worthwhile profit.

Some of what she sells comes from her own home and family, but the majority of her stock – which she 'warehouses' in a large shed at home – is given to her by the people she works for in her several part-time jobs.

'My stock is generally donated, and I'll build it up over the winter until I have enough to make a boot sale worthwhile. I usually have plenty to sell. If I've got stuff left over from the previous year, then I'll go through it all and see what I think I can still sell from it; the other stuff goes to a charity shop. This year, for example, I have a massive case of clothes that didn't go last year, and a lot of children's clothes, and that will form the basis of what I sell at the first one.'

BRANDS ARE KING/QUEEN

Kerry is quite open-minded about what clothing she sells. Women's, men's and children's; trousers, tops, jackets and coats; shoes, bags and accessories.

But the thing most garments require to merit a place in her sales display is a recognisable brand.

'Brands are very important, and if I inherit any item of clothing where the label's been cut out, then I know it's from a cheap shop, and probably won't get any interest.

'To give you an idea of what I find will sell, I would go for Top Shop, Marks & Spencer, Gap, Next, Punky Fish, and most of the sport and skater brands. Anything above these, label wise, then obviously that would be a yes too. Primark, to me, isn't special enough to put out.'

Nor do you need to be too slavish in following the prevailing seasonal outlook. Buyers at car boots tend to plan and think ahead much further than mind-in-neutral shoppers in malls and high streets. Summer sun or not, good stuff sells. 'Coats, for instance, always go, winter or not. If it's a good quality coat, somebody will buy it.'

With shoes, Kerry has a straightforward filtering method.

'I always think that if I wouldn't wear them myself, then I won't sell them. Anyway, I'll steam clean them before I either put them on myself or put them out for sale. I sold my wedding shoes like this, and I think I only ever wore them for about an hour anyway! Kids' shoes, especially if they're in good condition, will go very quickly.'

She's found all clothes for the tiniest of babies sell very fast but that, while girls' clothes are plentiful and do sell steadily, decent boys' clobber is harder to come by, and goes like hot cakes.

'Boys' clothes are very sparse. You don't find a lot of those because boys like rough and tumble and their clothes end up with holes in them, or covered in mud.'

Brands are important even where the items were originally freebies. Kerry found herself with eight Clarins make-up bags that had originally been giveaways with creams, and she sold them all to one woman who probably wouldn't have been interested in similar ones, even of a higher-quality material, if they hadn't carried such a luxury brand name.

Just like me, Kerry is not averse to taking any number of other items with her if she suspects they might have some sales mileage to them. And her findings about duffers are very similar to mine. Drinking glasses always come back unsold, and very few of the books she's ever offered have been bought.

'The one thing I can never sell is a metal candle holder, for some reason,' she says. 'Also, I've found that phone cases for older models are pretty much unwanted, and board games – no one seems to want those any more!'

CHAPTER 5

What you can and can't sell

You'll be relieved and perhaps not a little surprised to know that virtually nothing is outside the scope of a car boot sale in terms of what you are permitted to sell.

Just about any item you care to imagine can be offered to the public by a private seller, and the only restriction for most of us in this position will be what can feasibly be transported to the event in a car, a van or in a trailer.

It's a fair bet that if you're reading this book you're simply a private citizen with a determination to sell off some of your personal excess possessions, most of which will likely be second-hand. From an ease-of-selling point of view, this is great because it defines you as NOT being a trader. As an amateur vendor of your own stuff, or at least stuff you have been given for free, you can get on with the day and know that you are well within the law to raise and keep that cash.

We look at actually becoming a trader in some detail in Chapter 12. But here is some reassurance that, as a car boot seller, you are not one.

You aren't a trader if:

- You are selling only your own personal possessions.

- You are not selling items that have been bought for resale and profit-making, such as from another market, a wholesaler, a cash-and-carry, auctions or, indeed, privately.

- You sell alone, or with the voluntary help of family or friends – i.e. you don't employ someone to help you sell or assist you with the 'venture'.

- You sell at boot sales infrequently – every now and again. If you're there every week, come what may, and also flog goods at other markets, or from your home in a fully organised way, then you are considered to be a trader. Selling at a car boot on a regular, planned basis more than, say, every two or three months might also define you as a trader, although legally there is no hard-and-fast rule on this.

- Your income isn't significantly based on taking part in car boot sales.

The law, as I mention above, is pretty lenient on those private individuals who utilise car boots as a great way to de-clutter and recoup some dosh. But it hardens up considerably on anyone using this 'amateur' sales conduit for illicit business purposes.

The underlying reason for this is, of course, to clamp down on black-marketers who are slyly using car boots as a cash-in-hand way to earn their income and, of course, avoid paying tax on their profits.

So how exactly is this enforced?

'THEY' COULD BE WATCHING YOU

Well, staff from the Trading Standards departments of local councils make unannounced and subtle patrols of all car boot sales to keep tabs on proceedings. You won't be able to spot them because these officially appointed 'mystery shoppers' are in plain clothes and exercise a very light touch. They aren't doing this to persecute the little guy, but to clamp down on serial tax dodgers, some of whom might be linked to serious crime, fraud, 'fencing' of stolen goods and even money laundering.

In addition, undercover police officers sometimes patrol the bigger car boots when they have good reason to believe that the sales arena is being used for nefarious purposes. Once again, as a genuine private seller, you're extremely unlikely even to be aware of that.

Traders, as you will discover later in the book, are legally bound by a significant number of rules, laid out in various acts of parliament, to sell fairly, honestly and safely. If they fail to stick to these regulations, they can be open to prosecution and subsequently face some very heavy fines. And the fact is, if they are professional traders, they can't plead ignorance, because most of these rules are unequivocal and clearly defined. The fact is it should never be regarded as 'red tape' because most of it protects the seller as much as the buyer.

However, the good news is that most of it is irrelevant to the way a private seller might run his or her pitch. Genuine 'non-trader' sellers are mostly outside the scope of consumer law. There are, however, a few exceptions that you should be aware of, even if you know they don't apply to you.

YOU SHOULD TELL IT LIKE IT REALLY IS

The key is in the description of goods, whether written or spoken. You can't claim something is one thing when it isn't – say, when you describe an item as 'brand new and unused' when it actually has been used, or when you say some glasses are 'cut crystal' when you know they're moulded glass, or a jacket is 'leather' when it is in fact 'leatherette'. This applies just as strongly to authenticity and origin as it does to material descriptions. Moreover, suggesting or implying it's something it isn't and then saying it's 'sold as seen' is no get-out clause. If you're unsure whether the jacket is made from leather or the goblets are real crystal, you can say you 'believe' them to be but admit that you are not certain, so the buyers can make up their own minds on the merits of what they see and what you tell them. This isn't a charter to catch out anyone who makes a genuine mistake but rather a safeguard against misrepresentation – a polite way of saying lying!

If you do give a false description – even in error – then the buyer has an automatic right to either a full refund, or else a partial one to reflect the flaw and make the transaction fair.

Believe me, this protects you just as much as the customer. If you've sold, say, a set of hair curling wands and told the buyer, 'I've checked them and they're completely safe,' and then that person gets electrocuted, they can make a civil claim (as opposed to a criminal claim) against you for negligence. As well as personal injury, they might do the same for property damage.

You might feel that there could never be any consequence or comeback to dodgy selling, as you'll be packed up and away and never see the irate customer again. But it's best to stick to the rules and avoid any possible chances of conflict. And remember, anyone can write down the registration number of your car and, if they feel the need to, track you down.

And so we come to the two key items you are not allowed to sell:

- Stolen goods
- Imitation firearms

Aside, that is, from things for which you would obviously need a specific licence to sell anyway, such as alcohol, prescription medicines, hazardous substances, and actual firearms.

THINGS YOU REALLY SHOULDN'T SELL

Stolen goods

It should absolutely go without saying that you should not be selling anything stolen. Like, duh. But being the handler, rather than the thief, is almost worse. If it comes to it, the buyer will be getting their money back from you and not the person who stole the item in question. And the penalties – the fine and possible prison sentences

– can be even more severe for you than for the original, light-fingered culprit.

If you're legitimately selling things that are widely known for being pilfered from sheds and garages, such as a bicycle or a lawnmower, then you can always offer a receipt with your name and address on it as reassurance that the item is yours to sell. The same would go for a computer or mobile phone. You're not under any legal obligation to do that, but it means the buyer can be confident they aren't buying anything hooky.

Imitation firearms

This is another area where the law is clear. Under the Violent Crime Reduction Act 2006, and its strict supporting regulations, you cannot sell an 'imitation firearm' or a 'realistic imitation firearm' to anyone under the age of 18, and the offence would be similar for something like a BB gun. Any toy gun that is obviously a plaything because of its general look, lack of realism or size, should be fine. Advice from the Trading Standards Institute is that if you're unsure about any replica, imitation or toy gun you're thinking of selling, seek further advice from the police.

Trading Standards Institute (TSI) is the government agency that oversees all selling in this country. And it's very keen, while not discouraging enterprise in any way, to foster 'good practice' in private sales.

This leads to a handful of items that, while not illegal for you to sell, come with potential problems which mean they are probably best avoided.

Electrical goods

Sound advice to consumers would be never to buy used items such as irons, electric blankets or electric heaters and fires at car boot sales. This is because buyers can't be entirely sure of their source, condition or safety, and it would be foolhardy to give any solid guarantees along such lines against the potential dangers. Ask yourself: do you really want these things on your conscience? It would be best by far to avoid altogether taking them along to sell.

Food

You'll be committing a serious offence for which you'll be personally liable if you sell food that turns out not to be 'fit for human consumption'. Never mind that the labels may still bear 'Sell by', 'Use by', 'Best before' or 'Best before end' markings which haven't lapsed. Those markings can sometimes be dependent on consistent storage conditions. TSI does issue a leaflet entitled *Food Labelling – date and lot marking of packaged food*, which contains detailed information on the subject. Yet the fact remains that food selling is an area fraught with danger, and a car boot sale is not the place to offload packets and tins that you've had kicking around the kitchen for months but can't bring yourself to throw away. Make them something to avoid.

DVDs, CDs and other recorded entertainment formats

These, in a way, could also be considered as 'stolen' if they are illegal copies, because piracy is theft; theft of copyright in music, film or computer games. Even if you didn't do the copying, you can still be prosecuted for 'secondary infringement' under the Copyright, Designs and Patents Act 1988 if you're found to be selling duplicates for personal benefit, or even if you suspect they might be copies.

You'll be on generally safe ground if you're selling off your old DVDs, CDs, games and even cassettes, but you should be aware that films or videos you do have on your stall, no matter what the format, must have been classified for original release by the British Board of Film Classification (the official film censor). If you get caught selling something that was not 'passed' by the BBFC for UK consumption, you could be sent to jail and face a fine of £20,000 per film, under the Video Recordings Act. So take a look through your selection and chuck away anything that looks even remotely dodgy, rather than risk being pulled up during a random inspection.

Clothes

Don't worry: there is unlikely to be any issue with the vast majority of garments that you might take along for sale. But there are a couple of areas of apparel that are perhaps best left at home for disposal at a clothes bank.

The first is nightwear. Anything you buy new today from a reputable retailer will need to meet strict flammability standards, as indicated on the label. Can you be sure that yours are correspondingly safe? And if perhaps they didn't come from a known brand, did they meet UK standards in the first place?

The other area is children's coats and jackets with hood

cords. If you're uncertain of their provenance, or whether they meet safety standards related to the obvious hazards of entanglement, it would be a sound idea to discard them.

Cosmetics

The obvious point of conflict here is if the seal has been broken. If it's intact and unopened then fine, but if it's been partly used there is a real danger of contamination, especially if some of the ingredients are regulated materials. Once again, TSI has issued a leaflet on *Cosmetic Products*, which goes into the subject in close-up detail, but the official advice is that if you are in any doubt on the condition – and you can't give a cast-iron assurance to a potential buyer – then don't take it to a car boot sale.

Toys

There won't be many toys that were originally sold new in the UK that will present a problem. It will be more of an issue for toys that were originally sold outside the UK or, indeed, EU, or if you've got no idea where they came from or how old they are. If you still have them in their original packaging, that should help you to point out, for example, the minimum intended age they were designed for, and any instructions that came with them should be carefully and firmly attached.

Toys that are broken, with jagged edges or sharp points, or have small parts that come off when they shouldn't, or are frayed, worn or decayed in any way, should probably be chucked away rather than offered to the public.

EVEN MORE CAUTION REQUIRED!

There are a few items that you might consider disposing of at a car boot which are only sold new with very strict safety standards:

- Prams

- Pushchairs

- Children's car seats and boosters

- Bicycle and motorcycle helmets

- Paraffin heaters

- Oil heaters

In all cases, buyers would be crackers to buy these from a stranger at a car boot. So you ought to think long and hard before offering any of these items for sale. Once again, best not to even consider taking them along.

CHAPTER 6

The night before

Spending some time on preparation the afternoon or evening before the 'big day' is absolutely essential. It's an important part of the planning that will make your money-raising mission go smoothly. This way, you'll be able to easily connect and transact with every possible customer, and you will stay calm and unfazed as – hopefully – your sales bonanza gets off to a flying start.

My clothes-selling car boot expert friend Kerry Ball well recalls the first event she did, and how a lack of preparation nearly put her off for good.

'At the first one I ever did, I took my 14-year-old son with me, and I remember thinking I am never, ever going to do anything like this again,' she recalls with a shudder. 'I had no idea what I was doing, I didn't plan it out, I had people next to me, real pros, who had a great day – they sold loads and seemed to take a lot of money. At the end of it I felt quite stressed, and then I was just a buyer for a very long time.

'But since then, the more I've done it the easier it's got. I now do it on my own without a problem. And I cram as much into my car as I possibly can. But I always know exactly what I'm going to do, I know what to expect, I know what to put where and I know pretty much how things are going to turn out.'

THE FIVE CAR-PACKING RULES

1. Basic Principle
The overriding ethos here is to treat your car like a gigantic metal suitcase that has to be carefully packed so that its contents can be retrieved in the correct order.

2. Stacking Order
The first things you put into the back should always be the last things you need to take out, or the final convenience aid (as opposed to merchandise) you need before proceedings get fully underway, such as a fold-up chair or a cool box.

3. Don't Overfill
Make sure boxes can close flat, or that plastic stacking containers can indeed stack properly, and remember not to make them too heavy or you'll be at a real risk of a back or strain injury as you try to manhandle them in and out of the car.

4. Centre of Gravity
Only vary the previous rule if you have a mixture of heavy and light containers, making sure that the heavier stuff is at the bottom and towards the front of the load bay, with the lighter ones on top and/or at the back. The same applies for single larger items that you might be carrying loose. That way, things won't get crushed or move about in a

dangerous way if you need to perform an emergency stop on the way to the site.

5. Tables, Rails and Ground Sheets in Last

When packing the car, remember you're working backwards from the point of your initial sale. The first thing out should be the bones of your display, which in most cases will be a folding table, or two, that acts as your temporary shop display unit. But this might also include some plastic sheeting to protect your wares from dampness on the ground, as well as any other 'framework' item you plan to display or hang things on or in. If you intend to mount the Selfridges of car boot sales pitches, with rain and sun protection for your goods and for your customers, then this could include one of those foldout garden gazebos.

Vital recap: pack the car so the table goes in last and comes out first, and your items to sell follow in, roughly, the order you intend to set them out.

All of which sounds like a no-brainer, of course, but it's something that needs a good deal of focus beforehand.

HANG ON A MINUTE, YOU MENTIONED RAILS?

Let's assume you are one of the tens of thousands of Britain's car boot sellers who intend, like Kerry, to concentrate on selling clothes. Her advice on pitch layout has been a proven winner time after time.

'For me, it's all about hanging. And for that I need a rail. I have two of them, and I position them either side of my pitch, with two tables side by side in between. The left-hand rail has my children's stuff on it and the adult stuff is on the other, to the right.

'If you haven't got a rail, then you should really think about borrowing one from a friend for the day.

'In a shop, people wouldn't look through clothes if they were folded up in boxes. I know I wouldn't want to go through things that were in a pile, even if they were in a clearance sale; I'd much prefer a rack or a rail. Think about jeans: buyers are looking at both size and leg length. If they have to bend down and rifle through several pairs of jeans on a table or in a box, unfolding them and then trying to fold them up again, they're going to be put off, aren't they? If it was me, that would take too long. We're all in a rush at a car boot to get round as much as possible and I don't want to take ten minutes looking for what I want on one stall when I can find it easily elsewhere. If they're on a rail, then I can just flick through and move on. When you sell them on rails, they're doing the job for you.'

Sturdy but lightweight collapsible clothes rails are reasonably commonplace, and a modern one should be easy to assemble in a couple of minutes.

And if you really want to display your clothes with finesse, you could do like Kerry and make sure that everything hanging on that rail is washed and ironed. That way, customers will be surprised and delighted and, with any luck, feel emboldened to buy more than they thought they were going to from you.

BOXING CLEVER

If the haul you're planning to dispose of consists of a large number of small but solid and/or robust items – typical house-clearance bric-a-brac, toys, kitchen stuff and the like – then you can avail yourself of some of those tough cardboard trays that supermarkets give away once the fruit and veg stored in them has been sold.

They have two excellent material attributes: Firstly, they stack easily and neatly, and within a boxy car they are very space efficient. And secondly, they are strong but light.

But the best thing about them is that they can be pre-packed with a single layer of items and are then ready to spread out directly in front of the punters, either on tables or on the grass. If it's dry, they keep everything off the ground, and if it's a bit moist underfoot, then they should ideally be on top of a layer of plastic sheeting.

You can set out your items in these as if you were making up a hamper for a harvest festival display, grouping them together in zones or themes for best effect. With delicate items like china and glass, lay them in scrunched-up newspaper that will both pad them on the drive to the site and also help cushion items when people handle them.

I've done car boots where all my items have been packed in these. I was able to open the boot, put up the table, spread some sheeting on the space either side, and simply plonk down twenty to thirty of these boxes that were all ready-made displays of tempting odds and ends. Not much artistry involved, for sure, but it worked well for a swift, no-nonsense set-up.

Of course, you may want to unpack your bric-a-brac items and arrange them interestingly and individually on the table, which will make a more engaging display, for sure.

But it you're planning to have boxes of things on the ground as well, be certain to make sure they're neither too deep nor too cumbersome. A weak box that's subjected to too much burrowing and rough investigation will not only split or tear, but items will get damaged in the rummaging process

Wherever possible, try to think in terms of shallow boxes, for both transport and for display.

Plastic stacking boxes, of course, are fine, but they do tend to be deep and especially unforgiving when breakable things get jostled about inside them. They're great for softer items or for a small number of longer things whose ends can face upwards and still make an impact, but they don't always show what you have for sale to best effect.

A LOT OF SHOES? MAKE IT EASY TO TRY THEM ON

If you've got lots of footwear to shift, your potential buyers are going to want to try them on. In which case it might be a good idea to have a small stool or a small fold-up chair like a fishing seat so they have somewhere to do just that. If you've got something suitable in the house, take that with you, or borrow something from a friend.

A REALLY IMPORTANT QUESTION: TO PRICE OR NOT TO PRICE?

It really is not customary to have everything price-ticketed at a car boot. It isn't outlawed or anything; just not exactly the done thing.

I believe part of the reason for this is that most people simply don't have the time or the inclination. It involves getting sheets of price labels and putting a considered value judgement on every single thing you're intending to sell – which with a full car-load would be quite an undertaking. To price up everything might soak up an entire morning of your time.

More to the point, though, is that fixed, clearly marked prices can act as a major put-off to customers.

If you've been to one of these events as a browser, you'll know the excitement of picking something up and asking what the seller wants for it. You might be horrified at the ludicrous value they've put on it or, alternatively, you might be amazed and delighted that the sum is an absolute snip. If the price is already on it, then the seller is making a solid statement that that is the starting point for any negotiations. I know myself that I will quickly put something down that I find marked at a fiver, but which I'd anticipated paying £2 for, and walk off, convinced that the joker selling it just won't come down to anywhere near what I feel like parting with. In fact, in reality the person might have in a sudden fit of desperation decided to let it go at two quid. But that biro scribble on a small white sticker has acted as the deterrent to any bartering so much as getting airborne, much less cruising to a conclusion.

By all means have a rough idea of what you will take for things as a baseline. If you know those worn-once, still-boxed trainers cost £80 new, you will want to hold out for a decent price. Just don't let your zeal for order and neatness in the pricing department act as a barrier to prevent customers from choosing to engage. Pick your battles: have in mind the few high-quality items that you won't compromise too much on, and decide that everything else is to play for. Keep reminding yourself you are going there to sell on a one-off basis (for now, at any rate) and you want to end the day with, if not everything then, as much as possible of it in the hands of new owners.

My advice would be not to price.

Or only do so when the prices you chalk up broadcast positive quantitative *and* qualitative bargains, such as 'all items in this box just 50p', 'everything on the table £1' or 'designer tops, skirts and dresses all for £5 each'.

PACK IT IN

Once you've got a good idea what you're going to take, and it's all boxed up and ready to go, have the car completely packed up by 6 p.m. the evening before. You might as well fill every available inch of cargo capacity, leaving just enough space above your stock so you can see out of the back window using your rear-view mirror. You'll be setting off early, there won't be much traffic about, and you can always take it slowly and reacquaint yourself with your wing mirrors. Clearly, though, don't overload the car, making it dangerous because of the three anvils and two ships' anchors you want to sell. If you're unsure about your car's tolerance, check in its handbook and find out the maximum recommended laden weight. Chances are you won't even get close, as most cars can carry five adult bodies and all their luggage with no problem at all; you'll have two people and the rest of the payload as luggage, and even a heavily burdened car can still perform as it should.

GETTING YOURSELF READY

So, your stock is all loaded up and ready to go. How about you? You've got two areas to think about: the things you'll need to help you sell and the things it would be good to have to help you though a potentially hectic morning outdoors.

Your float

You'll be well advised to have a good selection of change with you to facilitate the early purchases. It's a great way to use up all those coins you might have lying around the house or maybe in the car. But if you have to go to the bank specifically to get change, I'd suggest £20 worth in the form of ten £1 coins, ten 50p coins and the rest in 10p and 20p coins. I wouldn't bother with copper, as I'm guessing you won't be pricing things up in factors of 1p or 2p, or indeed 5p, anyway. If my experience is anything to go by, you'll certainly be receiving plenty of copper, as buyers do tend to scrape the barrel and feel down the back of sofas for their spending money.

About £20 worth of coins should be all you need to get things started, but remember to have your organiser's pitch fee in additional cash so you don't give away all your float money at the gate.

Your 'till'

It's always a good idea to know in advance where you're going to put the money you receive from buyers. I see plenty of sellers with a moneybelt or 'bum bag' acting as a till drawer, and even if you don't use these, I'd strongly advocate keeping all your takings on you personally, perhaps in a dedicated coat pocket with a zip for coins, and notes tucked away somewhere close to you – say, a shirt breast pocket for a man.

I'd strongly avoid putting your takings in anything like a cash box, a Tupperware container, or a biscuit tin that sits towards the back of your table. Same goes for a handbag or sports bag on the ground, even if close to the car.

Don't plan to keep your money anywhere exept on you personally

Actually, I'd go further and advise against even a wallet that is constantly taken out of a back pocket.

Any slight distraction that means your eye is taken off your stash and it could be pinched. Practised sneak thieves will be well aware of anything that looks even remotely like a 'cash tin'.

Your packaging

Whatever you're selling, people love the offer of a bag. If you don't already have a load of carrier bags saved for reuse, then start gathering some in the days leading up to the sale day itself.

If you're going to be selling breakable items, then also make sure you have a stock of old newspaper for protective wrapping (no need to go mad and offer tissue paper bought specially for the purpose – it's a car boot, after all), and if you've been hoarding bubblewrap for no express use other than that it might just come in handy, take that along too. Not only do buyers really appreciate any protective wrapping for their new purchases, but while you are helping pack stuff up for them their eyes will be focused on your stock, and they may end up buying more.

Your outfit

When it comes to your morning's car boot work, there are two modes for which you need to be properly dressed.

The first is the busy first half-an-hour, when you'll be lifting and setting up and generally running around. Even though it will be chilly first thing in the morning, this will probably require some physical exertion, and it will be jacket off and sleeves up to get it done.

The second is the hours and hours of standing, and possibly sitting, while you man your stall. If it's a cold morning, this is where you might need some insulation.

It's all in stark contrast to the buyers, who are constantly moving as they work the field, and to a degree keep warm that way.

So make sure you have, for a cold day, plenty of layers, with an outer fleece, anorak or padded jacket or gilet to keep warm when you're just standing about and to see off any wind chill factor. For a really cold one, you'll also want a hat and maybe gloves. And, of course, thermals top and bottom.

And as there is to be quite a lot of going nowhere, you'll want your feet to be comfortable. A pair of supportive, waterproof walking shoes or boots is probably the best option, with trainers fine if it's dry and likely to remain so, and Wellingtons (with an extra pair of warm socks) if there's a chance it could be wet or muddy.

Of course, there is the outside possibility that the good old British weather on the day will be extremely hot and sunny. That could call for just shorts and a T-shirt, but remember that the spot you're allocated is likely to have very little in the way of shelter from a blazing sky. Sunburn might be a real possibility, no matter how much moving around you do as you attend to your customers. Don't forget your sunglasses, a baseball cap or sun hat and some sunscreen. If you know that you're going to have real difficulty lasting for six hours in hot, direct sunlight and sweltering temperatures, you might want to take a parasol or sunshade as a bit of relief should it get too much.

Sustenance
Pretty well every car boot sale has a smattering of refreshment 'concessions', although if you're expecting Pret A Manger or Costa Coffee, you will be sorely disappointed.

Organisers offer regular spots at their events to the owners of mobile snack bars and burger vans. These are much-coveted sites, as the majority of car boots are in fields well away from other retail snack outlets, and so there is a captive audience to exploit.

And 'exploit', in my opinion, they seem to do. Overpriced but poor-quality hot dogs, burgers, bacon rolls and other greasy delights are the staple cooked fare for anyone who suddenly gets an attack of the munchies, with a range of sweets, snacks, canned drinks and bottled water at prices usually comparable with railway station kiosks for their bloated cost.

It's the same with tea and coffee: you're asked to pay a minimum of £1.20–1.50 for a Styrofoam cup containing the cheapest of instant coffees or a meanly filled teabag and some hot water. A drink that would cost about 4p to make at home.

So take your own.

A flask of tea or coffee made how you like it, some water bought on the supermarket weekly shop, and some sand-wiches, cake, fruit or cereal bars purchased similarly. Bear in mind that it will be a long and quite possibly tiring morning, and you'll need the sort of regular bursts of slow-release energy that a cheeseburger doesn't give.

It's not just that my own food and drink will be more satis-fying and tastier than anything bought from a nearby caravan. It's that I am going to the car boot to make money and not to fritter it away on overpriced tiffin. Two of you could easily burn through £10–15 in this way, which might be a large bite of your final takings; fine to spend that if you see bargains elsewhere that you just have to have, but not on 'grazing'. Call me absurdly stingy if you like, but that is the focus I want to have. Besides, once my stall is set up and my stuff laid out for all comers to purchase, I'm going to be a self-sufficient shopkeeper. The last thing I want to do is waste selling opportunities because I'm queuing up for an expensive bacon sarnie…

AVOID POTENTIAL HEADACHES

I mean literally; for your first car boot sale there is a lot to be aware of and think about (but don't worry: you'll cope). So if you are prone to the odd headache, and assuming that these are your normal rescue remedies, pop a couple of par-acetamol or aspirin in your pocket, just so you have them to hand.

ARE YOU IN 'THE ZONE'?

Okay, so this is it; you've got everything ready – the right event for you, a car jam-packed with irresistible stuff to sell, a plan of how to set your pitch up fully formed in your mind and someone to help you. The weather's set to be fair, with only the outside chance of a shower. You've got the right shoes and a bagful of coins so you can give change to the first of the many buyers who'll be making a beeline for you.

There's no need to start humming 'Eye of the Tiger' or shadow-boxing an imaginary opponent; you don't need to take twenty extremely deep breaths.

But tomorrow morning you're going to take that car-load of clutter – everything you'll be glad to see the back of and won't ever miss – and because of your calm and thorough approach you're going to exchange if for a whole sack of cash. There will be a great sense of achievement and a proper monetary reward at the end of it all.

CHAPTER 7
On the day: arrival and setting up

By tradition, British car boot sales tend to start early on Sunday mornings – sometimes obscenely early. From this point on, I'll be discussing a Sunday morning event, as it's by far the most common example, although, of course, some boots are held in the afternoon and on other days too, for which all my advice can be easily adapted.

Many sites throw open their gates at 6 a.m., and none start later than 7 a.m. So you're going to have to be out of bed at 5 a.m., and maybe earlier still if you're going to make up fresh sandwiches, coffee and so on to see you through the morning.

However, I'm not convinced that there is any pressing need to make sure you're at the front of the queue. Being one of the very first to set up is probably a bit of a disadvantage, actually.

Car boot sale fields are arranged in long rows of cars parked end to end, with roughly a couple of metres spanning out from one side of the car that will constitute the floor space of your sales pitch for the duration of the morning. For a typical family car, that would be about 15sq m of ground, 20sq m for a large van, or maybe 24sq m if you happen to have a trailer attached to the car. Then there are grass corridors about 3–4 metres wide between the rows of stalls facing each other, down which the customers will be flowing.

You don't get to pick a position. That is usually decided on a first come, first served basis. As you arrive and join the line-up of sellers waiting to drive into the field, you simply take the place behind the vehicle in front. Organisers generally employ marshals whose job it is to wave your car into place and indicate when to stop. The upshot is that you're told where to park and once you're there that's it – that will be your world for the next five to eight hours.

HOW TO GET THE POSITION YOU WANT

I mentioned a couple of paragraphs back that being at the head of the pack isn't a good thing.

This is because you will find you are interwoven among the real diehard traders at the event. These guys are there every week, come rain or shine, and aim to be open for the longest time to sell as much of their standard stock – like tools or cut-price domestic products and refills – as they can. They are, if you like, hardened small businessmen, who often have regular customers that will always expect to find them at or near the beginning of row A. The only way they can assure familiarity of position is by getting there before anyone else. And, of course, in a way you've got to admire their discipline and acumen.

But as a private seller, I reckon it benefits you to be situated further along the early rows. If your pitch is midway down row B or C, then buyers will already have travelled up and down the aisles and be fully geed up, their purchasing juices fully flowing, if you will.

Anyway… stepping back a little… my recommendation is that you make a good early start without racing to be first. If your vehicle is somewhere between the fiftieth and the hundredth to arrive then you will have secured yourself, in my opinion, an optimum spot from which to trade. So if gates open at, say, 6.30 a.m., rocking up at 6.50–7 a.m. should serve you well in the bagging of such a position.

That said, you really don't want to get there late. I'd say that anything after 7.30 a.m. – maybe 8 a.m. at the very outside – and you've given away far too much of the prime selling time. Half an hour wasted early on is the equivalent of ninety minutes of late-morning selling time

The majority of car boots will be in full swing for the whole of Sunday morning, slowing down a little after 12 noon and dwindling markedly towards the end at 1 or 2 p.m. But, believe me, most of the big buying takes place early on, when the very keenest of buyers are focused and eager to strike deals.

This in fact, leads up to one of the most important moments in the chronology of the event – one of the factors that 'newbies' to this activity find decidedly unnerving.

You have, at this stage, been ushered into position by the marshals, turned the engine off, and you're on the cusp of getting stuck in. What now?

Do absolutely nothing

Because...

THE 'NIGHT PEOPLE' ARE CIRCLING!

The very earliest stages of a car boot sale attract an extraordinary group of motley characters who materialise as if from nowhere, like they've been sleeping in the trees and undergrowth until the first headlights flicker across the field to give them the signal to rise and swarm, zombie-like, as the pioneer vehicles draw to a halt.

These 'people of the night' are absolutely determined to have first dibs on everything that emerges from each hatchback as it's being opened by the unsuspecting seller. Like beggars in a Third World capital, they hitch themselves straight away to visitors and they don't care how intimidating they are.

Give it ten minutes

The moment you open the doors of your car, these folks, well padded from the cold in their thick coats and gloves, will be all over you and your stuff. By which I mean, when you open a door or tailgate, their hands will be inside, delving into your boxes and containers without permission. They really are very intimidating, and they'll bark, 'How much is this? How much is this?' at you in the most mannerless fashion. They're all over your stuff like a rash. As you start to unload, they will be virtually unpacking boxes for you, lifting and opening and unfolding and interfering before you've had a chance to gather your thoughts. A few, possibly, might seek to distract you so they can quietly filch something in the scrum.

It can actually be quite unpleasant. They are shameless in their drive to be first to root through your goods. And they are by no means the most desirable of customers anyway. They aim to bamboozle and confuse the unprepared, as you yourself might be, rushing them to make price decisions and generally hassling.

But there is a way round it. Just sit tight in the car for ten minutes, and bide your time. The night people might be tapping on your windscreen or scratching at your side windows to get at your gear but, as new arrivals start to park up in your wake, they will eventually tire of waiting and move on to the next new meat.

You are missing very little by initially staying closed to these ruthless strangers because their capacity for low offers is matched only by their ability to invade your personal space. I wouldn't say there is anything actually dangerous about them – they're just expert hasslers – but they certainly don't stand on parade and wait to be asked.

As car boot sale veteran Kerry Ball says, 'It doesn't matter that it takes time to set up, as you won't want to sell stuff to the very hard bargainers who are there right at the start. They want to pay the least.'

Once this torment has passed, it's time to snap into action for real. But there will still be plenty of interest in what you're about to put out – which is great, that's just what you want – so it's important to get those tables unfolded, those rails assembled and that plastic sheeting spread on the ground as soon as you can, and get cracking on unpacking and laying out what you have to sell.

PLANNING YOUR PITCH SPACE

From the get-go, people will be looking at everything you put out and starting to make offers left, right and centre. So make sure that as soon as you have your display surfaces ready you start filling them with items as rapidly as possible.

Try and unpack with a little bit of thought about what your few square metres of space is going to be like through-out the morning. Many people will choose to use their table, or even tables, as a sort of counter over which all transactions will take place and behind which the seller will stand or sit.

That does work well. But think about the layout. Is it actually putting a metaphorical barrier between you and the buyers? It could be better to arrange things around the edge of your plot, so that people enter the 'shop' and then have things to look at on three sides and maybe some items in the centre. You could position yourself at one end or even just mingle about in the central area so that you can keep a broad eye on everything.

Alternatively, you could have everything on tables that stick out at an angle to the car, so that customers can con-gregate on both sides of each table. Or else everything you have to sell could be in boxes and containers on the ground, around which people can walk and kneel down, dipping in at will. This certainly gives a no-nonsense image that will draw the ardent bargain hunters, but it could be off-putting to the elderly or those with creaky joints.

These are all ways to utilise the selling space and yet also provide enough room for customers to freely move around and access your merchandise. There are no wrong or right ways, and actually the very lack of uniformity around a car boot is part of the irresistible lure for buyers. What you have to sell may well influence how you position stuff, but decide early on how you feel this will work best for you, because once sales get cracking, you won't have much time for rearranging it all. Hopefully, anyway!

PRESENTATION IS EVERYTHING

Kerry has plenty to say about how you present your items to sell – particularly in the area of clothes, shoes and accessories. And it's marketing gold dust because much of it is based on her huge experience as a canny and discerning buyer. For instance, when she's doing her rounds in a buying capacity, she uses first impressions to constantly weigh up the potential rewards.

'There are some stalls that I won't even stop at because the seller has literally just chucked things on to the table,' she says. 'If they just throw it on there, then I'm sorry but I don't want to rummage – I don't look. How can you expect me to rummage when there are so many other stalls around where I can see everything easily? If I spend twenty minutes looking through this pile of clothes, I might be missing something great that's a little further on and is much easier to see.'

Her experience of both buying and selling is that, for adults' clothes especially, people are generally not willing to rifle through heaps of garments.

'People are naturally drawn to a rail, with everything washed, ironed and hung nicely. If they're displayed like that, then people will be happy to skim where they won't want to rummage. If you hang up a T-shirt that's been folded in a box, and it's not ironed, then it won't have 'kerb appeal'. If clothes are all crumpled, buyers might be wondering: "Have they been in the loft? Have they been in a shed? Are they slightly mouldy?"

'At a glance, I think things have got to give the impression they've been looked after. I think that's why my clothes go so well. If it has a mark on it, and I don't think I'd go for it myself, then I don't put it out.'

With children's clothes, browsers are a little more inclined to have a look through boxes and sort through a number of items that are on a table or in a plastic tub. Kerry's instinct would be to hang them, no matter how small the size, because they draw the right calibre of potential buyer.

'People like to dress their babies in beautiful clothes, and a lot of the stuff on sale at car boot sales is branded and good quality. So as long as there's something at the front of a rail that is obviously an expensive brand name, you'll get people looking through all of it.

'I do suspect that most of them are women looking to resell on eBay. I have a friend who does just that and is very good at it, because she's looking for brands that she can see are spotless but that still need to be washed and ironed to make them look really great.'

Why let these people take your profits away from you by not putting a little effort in? For the sake of a short time spent in preparing and showing them, you can charge more – £2 instead of £1, £5 rather than £3 – and grab some of that 'eBay profit' premium for yourself.

'I really made a big mistake last year with my children's clothes,' Kerry laments. 'I had loads of adult clothes to sort out, so with my children's stuff I just left them in a big box on the ground. I should have hung them up on rails. I would have sold much more, at double the price, if I'd done so.'

Kerry has some sage advice about sizes and ages. When she's perusing stalls at car boots, she finds she gravitates naturally towards sellers who are the same size as her – in this case, petite – because, in the split-second that she clocks the individual, she subconsciously recognises the similarity. 'I know that if she's in my kind of frame, then I might find something that I want to buy.'

Kerry turns this on its head when selling. Knowing that other women are likely to think in precisely the same way, and assume that she might have nothing to interest them in larger sizes, she makes a big effort to highlight the variety of what she's offering.

'If buyers come round and they do the same as me, and look at me, they're not going to look at my clothes if they're bigger than me. I have a lot of people asking me my size because I'm quite tiny. So when I do my rails I have a clearly written sign stating "12-up" midway along the rail itself.'

She does something similar on her children's rail, clearly delineating baby's, small children's and young teenager's material so that the choices are clear from 10 metres away as potential punters amble towards her pitch.

In the nicest possible way, you should also be aware of how old you look. Once again, buyers will take one look and make a snap decision, quickly computing your wrinkles and grey hair, or lack thereof, and deciding whether to call in or not.

'I generally take a look at the people who are selling, just as anyone else would at me, to see what they've got on and if they're my age group,' Kerry explains. 'If it's a girl who's twenty, she's going to have hot pants and vests and little things that I'm not going to wear. So why am I going to waste my time looking at things that aren't going to look right on me?'

The solution, once again, is to flag up with easy-to-read signs – capitals in waterproof marker on stiff card – the facts that you have, for example, lots of teenage clothes, or men's jackets, or garments more suited to the older or outsize lady, or indeed anything that you yourself wouldn't obviously wear (except for a fancy dress party). It might be a challenge to get the wording just right, but they could make the difference between getting your items noticed by the right target audience or just watching these prospective buyers sail straight by.

HELPFUL HINTS FOR IRRESISTIBLE DISPLAYS

There is one school of thought on how you present your car boot sale offerings that says that the messier and more disorganised it looks, the more people will be drawn towards the melee – the more they will want to root through the stuff on the hunt for overlooked treasure. But I think this approach is more to do with the possibility of taking advantage on the part of the buyer. As a seller, you're not interested in letting the buyers fleece you or take advantage of your ignorance. You're concerned with getting the best return, or at least a decent one, on your time investment in the event.

We've already discussed many aspects of what to sell and how to arrange your pitch. Now for a bit of fine-tuning for the really choice items.

Once again, Kerry's experience with accessories, shoes and home décor will turn browsers into multi-purchasers.

Accessories

If you're lucky enough to have plenty of disposable income, you might be using a car boot – much as you might a charity shop – to pick up one or two items that can enhance an outfit, or maybe you'll unexpectedly find a suit or dress that fits in with accessories you have already.

But what if you're using a car boot to source everything, maybe for an outfit for a party, wedding or a works do? As Kerry says, 'If someone is planning to go out and they haven't got much money, they might see one item with you, like a dress, and then start to look around for things from your stock to go with it.'

If you've got the right complementary items, make it easy for buyers to see them clearly displayed close to where the big-ticket items are hanging.

Kerry uses the back of her table for bags. These form a back-drop to other accessories, such as belts that are rolled up and placed together in a tray; matching colours, or those that Kerry thinks work well together, she puts close to one another. Items that are from the same brand she also places in close proximity to one another because, as she rightly points out, 'If, as a buyer I see someone has a brand name handbag, I know they've probably got a few more brands too, so I'll have a really good look.'

She will add shoes into the mix too, coordinating colours so that the eye is led easily towards them from other relevant 'pieces'. Well, I say 'them', but what I mean is 'it': Kerry has taken a leaf from proper shoe shops and only ever has one of any good pair of shoes actually on display and inviting inspection, as it might just be too tempting for a sneak thief to have access to a pair, and they'd go walkies. You can't trust anyone these days, can you?

Interiors

Kerry is a self-confessed addict for redecorating her home on a regular basis, like so many people across Britain. She likes to see the refreshing change it makes to the house . . . and you can be sure she has used car boots to source all manner of finishing touches that friends might never have suspected were achieved 'on the cheap'.

This hobby does tend to lead to last year's stuff needing to find a new home. And Kerry cleverly arrays in groups things like lamps, curtains and cushions that were once coordinated at home.

'So, for example, if somebody's looking for green, then they're drawn to that whole section of my items,' she explains. 'And nine times out of ten they'll buy several things at once.'

Apply this 'coordination rule' with all manner of groups of items, from tableware to garden tools and from ornaments to haircare products. Just take a little time to consider what goes with something else, and align them so that any seller can't fail to notice both. It's all part of helping the customer do the least amount of work and, ultimately, splash the most cash.

YOUR CAR LENDS A HAND

Don't forget you have a glass and metal backdrop – use it to good effect.

Okay, so it's not quite as beautiful as a gleaming chrome, glazed display unit from Monsoon or Zara, but your car itself has real potential in helping you sell.

It's parked across the back of your pitch the entire time you're at a car boot, and whether you use the roof rack, the roof rails, the tops of the doors, the tops of slightly open windows, or the double-aspect vertical/horizontal space on the bonnet or boot and wings, your car provides plenty of display space that can be put to very good use. The taller your car or van is, the more potential it has.

You can hang or drape clothes, coats, hats, curtains, bed linen and other soft furnishings from any of these vantage points, using decent coat hangers that won't damage your car's paintwork (i.e. not cheap wire ones). Use the metal space at the front or back to display things like rugs that can be thrown over the bonnet and boot and partly hang down over the front or back wings.

You could even place a few light but bulky items – such as baskets or lampshades – along the edge of the roof.

And if you're worried that they might get grubby from dust or mud on the car, then hang them in polythene, such as the covers supplied by dry-cleaners. As well as protecting them from marks, this will give the instant impression that the things are well looked after and definitely worth further investigation.

As most sellers tend to position themselves between the car and their display, then anything displayed on the car will be visible right next to, behind or above the storekeeper. Passing trade can't help but look at the seller, and then their eyes will naturally be drawn to everything framing them. If you've hung your own clothes on the car, your presence acts as an instant 'ready-reckoner' for browsers; if they can see it fits you, and they are about the same size, then it will probably fit them.

'I actually sold my wedding dress like this,' Kerry says with a grin. 'I hung it on the side of the car in its polythene bag and as people looked at me they saw the dress. I find hanging stuff on the side of my car really draws people in because it's at eye level. And once I've got their attention I can point them towards other things.'

CHAPTER 8

Learning how to sell

We've discussed all the many and various aspects of approaching a car boot sale beforehand, but now we get to the real nitty-gritty. How good a salesman or woman are you going to be?

Because you can, in truth, 'wing it' with much of the planning, and even be quite slapdash about your pitch, but still have a fantastically successful day as long as you can get all those potential customers eating out of your hand.

On that basis, think how well things are going to go with a combination of excellent preparation and good selling techniques!

YOU ARE HERE TO SELL

A short and ridiculously obvious statement, this, you probably agree. But this is still something you need to keep foremost in your mind throughout the whole of the car boot sale. It's all too deceptively easy just to spread out your items and then stand back to watch what happens. Do this and you may do all right. But add some verve to your selling, evolve your approach throughout the event and make a big effort to engage with every potential buyer, and you will almost certainly do considerably better.

READY...GET SET...BARGAIN!

From the very moment you declare yourself open for business, you are going to be assailed with offers. You will be put on the spot about prices, and you need to be ready to make almost continuous swift and decisive responses.

This is where, if you've carefully and dutifully price-ticketed all your items, you'll begin to realise that maybe it was rather a waste of time. Because whether the price is stated on paper or given by you verbally, in many cases it will only serve as the starting point for negotiation.

Among buyers at all car boots there are some shameless individuals. They will ascertain something is on offer for £5 and offer £2 or, when told that an item is £2, will say, 'I'll give you a pound.' Nothing is ever so cheap that they won't try offering half.

This is one of the key issues that rookie sellers get incensed about. Why are these people so impertinent? How can they be so rude as to make me such a derisory offer? Isn't the thing cheap enough already?

Well, you can huff and puff all you like about this but it won't make any difference. It is simply the stuff of life at car boots. And, what's more, buyers are fully entitled to make cheeky offers because second-hand goods, of course, have no set prices. You may not feel it at the time, but actually you should almost respect people for having a go.

For what people who consider themselves to be middle class, or comfortably off, can easily forget is that car boot sales provide a vital way for the very poorest in society to enjoy some of the materially good things in life, at a fraction of the cost they would command new. They're making offers because they're a few steps up from penniless, and they are trying to make their limited finances stretch as far as they possibly can.

But, of course, there are also those not on the breadline who routinely bargain for an even better price. They regard it as part of the game at a car boot, intrinsic to 'the sport', and feel that no price is a good price unless it's been chipped down by at least a third, and maybe more.

After all, nearly everyone twigs that car boot sellers in the main want to unload as much of their car-load as they can. Savvy buyers can depend on that imperative to stick their necks out and have a wrangle over just about every price that's quoted.

Somewhere in the middle of all this, the right compromise can be found. The buyer can play it cool, you don't need to come over as too needy, and a price can be struck. It's a mind game where both sides generally well understand the score from the off.

DON'T GET MAD, GET EVEN
Rather than get resentful about hard bargainers, embrace the tussling involved. Take pleasure in the haggling process – get into the swing.

Be prepared to listen to all offers, and perhaps be ready to give a little more than you initially wanted. But know when to give the impression that you've heard enough and that, unless the buyer is willing to go for the last figure you suggested, the deal's off.

On no account get shirty with your tricky customers – if proceedings end on a sour note it might jeopardise a successful resumption of negotiations minutes or even hours later. Just be firm, and don't take any of the bargaining assaults personally; this is meant to happen.

...But remember (I may have mentioned this before): you're here to sell.

You've made an enormous personal effort to be at the car boot sale today, and the primary objective of all your hard work is not just to exchange your unwanted possessions for cash, but also to end the day with substantially less to take home than you arrived with.

Keep that firmly in mind when you're reaching the end of your tether with someone.

On the one hand, they're fraying your nerves with an offer that is getting close to derisory. But on the other, the item could be big and bulky, a real millstone that you don't want to have back on home turf.

A good example of this might be a baby's cot – an expensive one, fancy, nicely made, wooden and all that. Your kids will never need it again, none of your friends wanted to take it off your hands for a 'drink' or for free, but you just can't get it out of your mind that the thing cost you £150 new. It's spotless and attractive and you're asking £40 for it, but now this insolent character standing here in front of your pitch is offering £25.

This is the sort of situation where, in truth, and based on a set of figures like this, you need to put your pride aside, paste on a big smile and say, 'Okay'.

You may feel in your heart of hearts that you'd prefer to hold out, because someone else is bound to come along and pay you £30–35. But it might just be that this is the only person here today who will actually step forward and pay anything at all for it. It's getting close to half-price, for sure, but here is a customer ready to buy it. AND…it is big, and you don't want to take it home because once it's reinstalled there you're back to square one in terms of clutter and a disposal plan.

A scenario like this is something to bear in mind with just about anything you have for sale. If you have no immediate plans to do another car boot, your overriding philosophy to it should be:

Close the deal

Endure the insult of the offer, but sell the thing anyway! Keep reminding yourself that a car boot sale is the freest market environment in the country, where everything is up for grabs. If several sellers have similar wooden cots but there is just one person at the event who's looking for one, then make sure it's yours that sells and not somebody else's. Holding out against the hardest of bargainers may make you feel strong, but it might just defeat the object. You set out specifically to sell your items, so don't let any potential sale escape you.

IT'S BIG, IT'S SOLD, BUT IT STILL DRAWS 'EM IN

If you have something bulky on your display, you may find it attracts a buyer early on who is happy to pay for it but asks to collect it later. This is fine; negotiate the deal and pocket the money, and then perhaps slap a 'SOLD' label on it.

Indeed, this can act in your favour. A large item that stays in your display despite being sold can still lure people in. They can't help but be drawn by something prominent.

'If someone has bought something and they're going to come back for it, I'll still keep it within sight but next to me,' says Kerry. 'If people like it, I'll say, "Sorry, it's sold," but it might make them keep looking at my other things. I had just such a situation recently with a child's bike. It had a value as a sales tool even after it had been reserved.'

GETTING A LITTLE BIT PROACTIVE

However they choose to navigate their way around the events, your set-up will be on most people's routes. One way or another, pretty much everyone who's attending is going to trundle by, and their eyes are going to linger, no matter how fleetingly, on your pitch. Here are a few hints on how to make the most of the 'window' of their attention; I've found these really work in keeping potential customers lingering in the environs of my merchandise.

• Say 'Hello' or 'Good morning'

Seems like such a basic communication but it should pop out almost instinctively the moment you make friendly (as opposed to hostile) eye contact, and as long as the response is similarly cordial you can follow it up with, 'How are you?' A little bit of ice will have been broken, the browser will feel you are friendly, and then suddenly the intensity of her or his gaze will harden as they begin to examine what you have more carefully. Don't be self-conscious; they won't think you're some sort of slimy insurance salesperson or anything like that. It just focuses them on you as a polite and approachable seller. Kerry Ball sums it up perfectly: 'If you engage, people stand there longer, which means their eyes are roving.'

• Your body language

Scowls and crossed arms have never done much to welcome people in. If you look defensive and unapproachable, then you're putting unseen barriers up between you and possible purchasers. Smiles really help.

• Notice what they're looking at and point out other similar things that might appeal

You know exactly what you have on your pitch but the prospective buyer might not be able to see the wood for the trees. So, for example, if a woman is having a good look at shoes, point out that you have a coat or handbag that would match; if it's a man examining a fishing rod, point out the accompanying bait box that he doesn't seem to have noticed; if it's a teenager looking at a guitar, say that you also have a pile of sheet music and a box of plectrums. It's well worth highlighting even the most vague synergy between items. It alerts people to things they simply didn't notice, and establishes the fact that you're looking to do a deal…which, of course, you are.

• If something has an honest fault, point if out
If your buyer is looking closely at something you know has a problem, flag it up before they have a chance to notice it. Kerry suggests small yet easily remediable issues on clothes are the sorts of things to mention. 'If there's a button missing, or a jumper has a little snag in it, then I'll point them out. It won't put people off if you can show that it's something they can fix.' It might be the same with tools or kitchen gadgets or, indeed, just about anything. If you know there's a blemish or something missing, make a point of saying so. If things do have battle scars or damage, they're not going to make big money anyway, and the buyer will pick up on the fact that you're very much in the market for an offer that reflects the fact.

• Keep your pricing simple to cope with the rush
A multiplicity of specific prices, especially if you're holding all the information in your brain, is going to lead to a spinning head if you're suddenly under siege from customers all asking 'How much is this?' So keep your prices simple where you can. 'I keep my prices the same for similar things – all tops the same or all jeans the same,' says Kerry. 'Someone might hold something up [at the other end of the stall] and I don't want the confusion of remembering different prices if I give a price.'

• Indicate your willingness to sell in bulk
Seasoned car boot buyers will simply assume that you are

well up for an offer on a bunch of items. Still, make your willingness to negotiate on a job lot known. The customer is looking at one or two of your china ornaments or jigsaw puzzles, so tell them that you'd be happy to hear what they might offer you for several of them. It opens up buying possibilities in the mind of the buyer, yet also puts the ball firmly in their court to consider what they might like to walk off with at a killer price.

• If someone likes one of your things, chances are they will like others

By and large, anyone who picks up anything from your stall is going to share something of your taste. By engaging them in any way in conversation, you're slowing down the speed with which they move on, and keeping them scanning and re-scanning your items. Of course, there is a balance to be struck between being friendly and being overbearing, but in my experience chat and interaction over items on sale frequently leads to them changing hands, so grab the opportunity to make connections and make the punter gravitate towards you. A repeat customer is usually the best kind, and many buyers will make a point of returning to any stall they liked on their initial tour.

• 'What a lovely dog'

Eh? Well, dog-lovers seem to make up quite a large proportion of car boot visitors, presumably as the two activities of browsing and the daily walk can be combined in one pleasant outing. I'm not sure how enjoyable the mutts themselves find trailing round piles of unwanted human junk but, then again, there are always plenty of other pooches to sniff (and occasionally to lunge at). Owners love it when you compliment their pets, tending to hang around to chat to you. This frequently leads to a reciprocal interest in your wares, and sometimes a few extra sales. Female sellers might also compliment a cute baby or cheeky toddler in the same way to establish a rapport with a fellow mum, although this would probably come across as a bit creepy from a man.

Okay, so I know you might recoil from some of these suggestions. But hopefully you get the idea. Things can sell themselves but you may be able to shift so much more if you establish interaction with the target audience. Any car boot sale is a competitive field, and in general the more you do to make doing business with you a pleasurable experience, the more you'll sell.

MAJOR NO-NOs

As a frequent car boot visitor myself, I see plenty of what you might term 'bad practice' from sellers. Here are a few of the things I notice and despair at, and that you ought to avoid.

• Sitting inside the car

Instead of being in and around their stock, or standing behind their counter ready to serve, some sellers demonstrate their default repose as sitting inside the car, sometimes with the window closed and sometimes apparently totally indifferent to the proceedings outside as they tap away on their mobile phones.

• More interested in gassing than selling

This often involves a couple of selling friends, who seem to be using a car boot as an opportunity to catch up on gossip. People, including myself, are sometimes trying in vain to get a word in edgeways, or attract attention. What can they be thinking by being so inattentive?

• Frazzled family aggro

It could be hubby and wife having an ongoing snipe-fest, or it could be mum chastising children. Either way, family grief of whatever kind is not conducive to pulling in the buyers.

• Display in tatters

After an hour of intense examination by punters, your stand can become a bit dishevelled looking, as people have turned over, knocked down and generally mixed up your items and left the place in a mess. You as storekeeper should be using any spare moments to resurrect your display and keep it looking attractive. Analyse your line-up, rearrange items, bring former 'background material' to the fore to take up vacated space; shake things up, don't just sit there wishing and hoping.

This is maybe where, as mentioned previously, having clothes that people need to unfold to inspect can be annoying. It's soon a mess of discarded fabric arms and legs. 'You've got to take the time to put things straight,' Kerry says. 'During the time you spend sorting it out you're not on the ball when people are looking at your other things.

'If you don't do it, it looks too messy, and people won't buy. It's a catch 22; I don't want my back to people while I tidy up because I should be facing them and saying good morning, how are you, and so on. It's never good to have your attention away from customers.'

• General resentfulness that the buyer is a profiteer

A significant number of people who regularly attend car boots are out to make money themselves. They have specialist knowledge and they're using it to winkle out gems that they intend to sell elsewhere, either online via auction sites like eBay, via antique shops and auctions, or through other specialist conduits with which they are very familiar and skilled. It could be as simple as looking for pieces of expensive-when-new clothing with good brand names, or as esoteric as recognising a lost work by a renowned painter, and all kinds of rare, interesting and collectible things in between. Indeed, I've been just such a buyer many, many times myself, as I know a great deal about a few narrow specialist areas.

As a seller, you should never resent people like me. Don't seethe. After all, you've brought the stuff along and, if you suspect that certain things might be hyper-valuable, you could always have used that thing called the Internet to do a quick check and then sold it through a more rewarding channel. Collectors and dealers don't make money easily; they really have to put in the legwork to find their hidden treasure. So don't get snotty with people who you suspect might be looking for profit. They're generally only exploiting other people's laziness.

• A fat lot of use that information is!

I admit it, this might just be a personal gripe, but there is nothing quite so annoying as a seller who has what you want but hasn't brought it along. I've lost count of the number of times I've picked up something interesting and asked the vendor the price, only for him or her to add that they've got loads more like it at home. Why the hell didn't you bring them, then! I don't want to know what's not available to me, now, do I?

CHAPTER 9
Difficult situations for sellers

There are two main sets of problems likely to be thrown at you as your car boot sale event progresses: one lot comes from nature and the other arises from contact with your fellow men (and women). The first you can definitely make contingency plans for – the second is a whole lot less easy to anticipate in advance.

THE WEATHER
Whether you live in Lancashire's rain-soaked north-west or the balmy English Riviera of Devon, you'll never be entirely able to predict how the elements will treat you.

The main adversary, obviously, is rain.

Most of us will still want to press ahead with our morning's selling if only slight drizzle or the outside chance of a shower is forecast. The more solid and generally 'hard' the items we have to sell, the less we will care about a light downpour. I've been to a few rural events where most of the goods on sale were old tools and garden stuff, and when it chucked it down no one seemed to mind too much; sellers and buyers mostly sported wellies and waxed jackets anyway, and little of the stuff on sale seemed to suffer unduly in the resultant soaking.

The problem for the rest of us from mostly urban and sub-urban homes is that much of the merchandise we will be selling will be 'soft', i.e. made from fabrics or paper, and not best disposed to a drenching.

Ideally what you need is a section of thin plastic sheeting to hand that's big enough to cover your entire display in one deft throw if storm clouds arrive. To have this folded up and ready to deploy in the car won't take up very much space, and it should be an easy task for two of you to throw it over everything in the event of a major cloudburst.

If you can get clear or opaque plastic – rather than bright blue, black or other solid colours – then that is all the better because ardent booters, who will not be deterred by a bit of rain, will still be browsing and will want to see the measure of what you have in spite of the prevailing conditions. So don't disappoint them.

Just remember that the sections of the sheeting that hang down over the edges of your table or end at the outer reaches of your pitch will act as conduits for the rainwater, leading to pooling and puddles. In the rush to protect your goods, make especially sure that water isn't running off and sploshing over vulnerable things.

More specifically, when the first drops of rain are felt, rush to protect anything made from paper or cardboard. That would include books and magazines, games and jigsaws, and absolutely anything that you are selling in its original packaging. These items, on a sunny day, are naturals to lay out on the ground to attract people's attention, but they can quickly become a sorry, soggy mess when they get wet. Gather these things up and usher them towards shelter as fast as you can.

As a regular book-buyer at car boots, I've often been dismayed to come across rare and interesting books that I might have paid good money for but that have been allowed to get wet – sometimes from rainfall but also on occasion from heavy dew on wet grass. It's a shame for saleable things to get damaged when it could have so easily been avoided.

Seasoned seller Kerry adds that you need to act quickly with anything featuring a plug. 'Electrical equipment would go straight into my car if it rains, as it looks very bad to have it on sale when wet.'

She, like me, is also well aware of the negative effect that mud can have on your pitch. Conditions might be muddy when you arrive, or become muddy with the passage of the buying public or the aftermath of a rain shower. If mud is in the vicinity, like as not it will make its way on to your display if you have things laid out on the ground. A plastic sheet spread out to act as a barrier between your goods and the damp ground is one thing, but if people walk over it in their muddy shoes, it can soon look dreadful.

'You can put a sheet down but if buyers want to get something from the back, they've got to climb over all your stock. You're behind your table, so you might not be able to get it for them. This can be terrible when it's raining or muddy, and things get trodden on. I think it looks bad and puts people off.'

Wind

A strong breeze, especially if accompanied by a swirling rainstorm, can play havoc with your display in any number of ways. Just make sure that whatever you have for sale is well positioned not to act as any kind of sail should conditions be windy, as a strong gust could end up overturning several things and perhaps tipping them into mud, where they'll be rendered unsaleable. No one is going to buy a hat for a wedding after it's flown through the air and landed in a puddle, now, are they...

Sun

Well, this particular type of weather shouldn't present too many problems for anyone. The only downside might be that the blue skies and warm rays send customers a little bit crazy, and in the heat and clear light they start to literally fight over what you're offering. Wouldn't that be great? Well, no, probably not, because no one really likes the British public when it gets frenzied and loses its cool. And that is apt to happen at a car boot sale as much as anywhere else.

YOUR GUIDE TO TRICKY CHARACTERS

The tough bargainer, I reckon, you are already well prepared to face. But there are a variety of other types you might encounter who will test your tolerance.

Thieves

Nicking is probably the biggest menace at car boots. The events are bound to attract the light-fingered, the pickpocket and the serially deceptive because they are largely made up of amateur sellers, a vast array of small items are on sale and security measures are, by the very nature of the layout of your things, lax at best. The temptation is simply too great. Having said all of that, it constantly surprises me that I find time and again the overwhelming majority of British people are very honest, and would no more think of stealing anything than they would engage in physical violence.

The surest way to protect against stealing is to have one person selling and the other keeping watch. With a small table, obviously, that is fairly straightforward, but once you've extended your aspirations with two tables and stacks of other items on the ground around them, it's easier said than done.

Try to keep your small and/or high-value items close to where you know you'll be standing throughout most of the event, with the larger and cheaper items at the perimeter of the pitch. Kerry points out that jewellery and watches are frequent targets for a lift. 'They will go, given half a chance,' she says, 'and I'm always a bit suspicious of people who spend a lot of time umming and ahhing. I have this feeling that they are playing for time, maybe hoping that my attention will eventually be taken away from them so they can pocket it.'

Of course, the older and more worldly wise you are, the more sensitive will be your antennae to likely pilferers. You will just get that funny feeling that the person rummaging and yet also glancing at you shiftily from time to time has devious intentions. You will keep visual tabs on them until they either wander off empty handed or else confound your expectations and buy something from you in a seemly manner.

Sometimes, thieves operate in pairs. One causes a distraction and, while your attention is diverted, the other makes off with something. It's an old trick but one that works. Once again, the only real answer is to be a good double act with your selling companion. Discuss this scenario on the way to the event or while you're setting up, and try to be prepared – jointly – to keep an eye on any dodgy-looking duo that comes your way.

Some thieves can be unbelievably sneaky. Kerry relates the tale of her job lot of wash bags. An apparently upstanding lady asked her how much they were. A pound each, came the reply. Then when Kerry turned away to serve someone else, the lady stuffed four bags into one and then proffered her £1 coin. Only Kerry's quick-wittedness uncovered the attempted robbery. The lady then simply unpacked her swag, paid for one and walked off, with no apparent qualms.

In this case, tackling the ne'er-do-well sorted the issue out. But is it really a wise move to tackle someone you suspect of stealing?

If someone grabs something and simply legs it at an athlete's pace, you are in an impossible position, because you won't be able to abandon your stall to give chase. The best you can do is to give a description of the person to the organisers afterwards, although how that would help you to recover your stolen property is a moot point.

If you see someone put something of yours into their bag or pocket and there is a chance to apprehend them, that also presents its own problems. At issue is the fact that you can never be entirely sure how a stranger will react if challenged. I used to spend the occasional morning helping out in my local hospice charity shop, and the official policy emphasised frequently to the volunteer workforce was that thieves should not be challenged because they could turn out to be violent. As most of the things we sold were donated anyway, and therefore represented a zero cost to the organisation, it was simply not worth the risk of having a knife pulled on us or being shoved, punched or kicked. We just had to let it go, and console ourselves that a) they have to live with themselves after stealing from a charity shop, and b) plenty of decent folk put all their change into our collecting tin anyway.

Perhaps that is, ultimately, also the best approach with theft at a car boot. Make your very best efforts to deter theft by being vigilant but, if something does get pinched, don't put yourself in possible danger in an attempt to thwart it.

One thing you can definitely do, though, to ensure your property does not go missing, is to keep anything valuable – and especially handbags or holdalls with your personal items inside them – inside the car with the doors locked and the windows fully closed. In this way your car acts as your strong room and should be unassailable. If the doors are unlocked, or open, then it is all too easy for the uninvited to saunter round the back while you're busy selling and help themselves.

Timewasters

It is amazing that some people appear to go through everything with a fine-tooth comb and yet buy nothing.

Or they try on and take off half a dozen items of clothing with, seemingly, no intention of choosing one, and head for the metaphorical checkout.

Or they ask you a dozen questions about something, examine it, debate it, screw you down to a giveaway price and yet still don't reach into their pockets.

It is supremely frustrating to deal with people like this. You could almost give them the thing for nothing and they would find a reason to still say no.

Selling to individuals at a car boot is a hit-and-miss business at the best of times, but the places seem to be paradises for the timewaster. You just have to try to let it wash over you. Imagine that you are an Oxford Street department store with a New Year sale on, and that a good half of the people who come in and finger the merchandise are simply tourists who are killing time. You can't prevent them from browsing and nor can you get angry with them for doing so. You just have to hope that, among them, there are one or two who can't stop themselves from making an impulse purchase.

The unappealing

Remember, this is the general public you're facing, and it takes many forms – not all of them savoury. Among Sunday morning shoppers are all kinds of people. Some of them have abrupt manners, some are uncouth and/or loud, some might have overpowering personal odour issues, and yet more could have a brood of annoying children in tow. Whatever it is that attracts or repels you about 'other' people, it must all go on the backburner while you're selling, because they're all potential customers.

Actually, some of the oddballs I've encountered at car boots have turned out to be very good buyers indeed and, despite appearances, very decent people with whom I've had some interesting chats. So you can't really afford to be too judgemental. Try to make everybody equally welcome and valued at your pitch. Er, apart from…

The Rabbiter

There is a certain type of person who sucks your selling lifeblood from you when you should be devoting your attentions to cash-flashing buyers. I call him (for it almost always is male) the Rabbiter.

This is the person who fixates on something you have for sale but, rather than have a quick natter and then purchase it, uses the thing as a hook to bore the pants off you. This usually takes the form of long and rambling descriptions of similar things that he has at home or is looking for or his friend owns or that he's modified/improved/sold/coveted.

Generally, although your face has a flashing yet invisible sign hanging above it stating 'I'M NOT INTERESTED. OK?', people like this don't get the message. You are not here to be a new best friend; you are here to sell. While trying not to be rude, you do need to be prepared to cut such a Rabbiter short, zone out from the tales of his fascinating life and attend to other customers. Hopefully, there will be plenty around to yank your focus in their direction.

Passive-aggressive body language

I was wondering how I could sum up this particular mode of behaviour from buyers, which I have experienced twice when selling. And I think the above, presently trendy psychobabble buzz phrase fits the bill quite well.

Person comes up to my table, picks something up, inspects it and demands to know the price. My reply is £3, whereupon the browser promptly slips the item into the bag he's holding before saying, 'I'll give you £1.'

Now I'm in a tricky corner, and the cunning shark knows it. He is, in effect, holding my item to ransom, and for me to grab it back means that I'd be forced to invade his 'personal space'. I think most people would agree that is a line you'd think twice before crossing.

I admit that the first time this happened to me, I was so shocked that I agreed to the offer after a bit of verbal to-and-fro. It hacked me off no end afterwards. When it happened a second time on another occasion, with two of us manning the pitch, one of us went round by the person's (a woman, this time) side, and the need to get stroppy with her was removed when she came up with an offer we could reasonably go for.

It doesn't happen routinely. But when it does, I feel you need to make a quick decision to get rid of the person as quickly as possible. If you don't feel you want to get combative, it might be better to let the item go at the insulting price. If, however, collectively you feel you have the looming presence to intimidate in return, then one of you – preferably the one who looks most like a nightclub bouncer – will need to look like you definitely won't be pushed around. But fight shy of any actual physical stand-off where you can.

The mark-up brigade

Another all-too-familiar character prowling around at car boots is the habitual seller looking for items to buy cheaply in one part of the event and then sell at a mark-up or increased price on his or her own stall in another area. Actually, they don't have to be far away; I've had cheeky blighters with a pitch a few 'doors' away and, once, even right next to me, who've worn me down on price and then set 'my' items out for resale and profit.

Do you know what you can do about this? Absolutely nothing. Because, of course, you are free to do exactly the same if you want to. If you have the nous and the knowledge, you can buy from others to sell at a fat profit too, and they won't be able to do anything other than grumble about it. In any event, that kind of buyer takes the risk – perhaps they won't be able to shift it, but at least you have. Think of the car boot sale as similar to the European Union. We find it outrageous that the French, the Poles, the Italians and the Spanish can come over to this country and buy a house, send their kids to school here, and use an NHS hospital if they break an arm. But we are actually free to do just the same in their countries, if only we can work out a way to make it feasible.

The mark-up brigade do tend to make their rounds early, like most of the 'pros'. If you think you have good stuff, don't be too eager to give it away in the earliest hours of a boot. And it almost goes without saying that if you let things go for a song, you only have yourself to blame. There's not much you can do about that, other than not to worry about it – the market can be cruel, and you should have held out for more money!

BREAKAGES SURE DO HAPPEN

Whether it's down to you as you unpack and set out your delicate items, or the buyers as they pick up, examine and put down those same things, it's almost inevitable that things will be damaged or broken from time to time.

China, pottery and glass are the most obvious candidates for getting chipped, cracked or smashed when dropped or knocked against something else. I've also found that glazed pictures of almost any size tend to be exceptionally vulnerable, cracking at the slightest provocation even in the most careful of hands.

If you break something yourself, that's just too bad, you butter-fingered so-and-so. If a punter breaks something, though, what power of redress do you have?

Most sellers, assuming that the item was priced at a pound or two, will make a quick and philosophical decision to shrug it off and, with a look of resignation, probably tell the clumsy punter not to worry about it. This is probably the best approach. It could be uncomfortable to try to force the person to cough up the asking price in compensation. The best way might be to suggest they buy something else from you at the same value. On the other hand, and taking a positive view of human nature, many decent folk will likely pay anyway because they'll feel too guilty about not doing so.

On balance, if you do offer some largesse it's quite likely – I've certainly found this – that they will feel obliged to buy something else from you anyway. In fact, on at least one occasion for me, something cheap got broken but the culprit then bought another item that was quite a bit more expensive, so the breakage became a sprat to catch a mackerel.

What often happens is things get damaged or broken without you ever noticing. It either happens unknowingly or else the rummager is too sheepish to fess up and quietly slinks away, leaving the wreckage behind them.

The fact is that if you have too many items thrown together in a box, this is almost inevitable. As mentioned previously, shallow boxes where items are arranged next to one other, as opposed to on top of each other, are the best way to ensure this doesn't happen.

DON'T HURT YOURSELF

This will barely apply to anyone selling clothes and toys, but if you're trying to shift tools, DIY materials, car components, machine and electrical parts, old tins of substances like paint, and even cutlery and kitchen implements, you do need to be aware that these things can cause injury to potential customers as they pick or rifle through your goods. And never more so than when they are rusty or have damage that results in an unexpectedly jagged profile.

My feeling is that the majority of adults who appear to know what they're looking for – and you can probably tell immediately, for example, if it's a self-employed tradesman searching for tools for his job – should be aware that their hands are going to come into contact with sharp points and edges. It might be less obvious to an old lady sorting through a box of old cutlery, among which there might also be kitchen knives, skewers and graters lurking. So if you see an 'amateur' about to innocently dive in, it's perhaps best to give a word of warning about what lies there.

Similarly, an awareness of what can happen if you tread on a rake (you know, how the handle can fly up and smack you in the face) should be your impetus to carefully arrange garden tools and other implements which might prove hazardous when stepped on or tripped over. No one is suggesting you need a diploma in Health and Safety, just a sensible approach as to how you arrange things that might prove harmful if people come into accidental contact with them.

FIRST-AID KIT?

You don't need to take the whole shebang; but it might be a good idea, if you are selling old tools, to have a couple of plasters and a small tube of antiseptic cream in your personal bag. For you if not a buyer.

MONEY MATTERS

For many car boot sellers – maybe the majority – handling money from customers can turn out to be quite a novel experience. After all, most of us have our salaries paid direct into our bank accounts, with very few workers these days receiving the traditional brown envelope of notes on a Friday evening. What's more, the country has moved over wholesale to making payments even for small items with debit cards. It's entirely possible these days to have a virtually cashless lifestyle.

Nevertheless, car boots drag you back to the good old days of filthy lucre. There may be one or two professional traders who are geared up to take credit and debit cards, but they remain in the absolute minority.

Everyone who buys from you will be paying hard cash.

And I've never come across a seller who baulked at receiving dosh in whatever form it's handed over.

The law states that you are not legally entitled to offer change, as it's up to the buyer to pay the exact figure, but like everyone in the UK, you are bound to accept certain notes and coinage because it is legal tender. These are the official rules:

- In England and Wales, Bank of England £5, £10, £20 and £50 notes are legal tender for payment of any amount.

- Notes issued in Scotland and Northern Ireland are not legal tender anywhere (Scotland included), but they are widely accepted as legal currency, and can be exchanged at almost all banks and Post Offices for English notes.

- No banknotes are accepted as legal tender anywhere in Scotland, down to the different legal status of sterling there.

- Coins are legal tender throughout the whole of the UK, Scotland and Northern Ireland included.

- Official legal tender rules stipulate that you have no alternative but to accept 1p coins in a quantity up to an amount of 20p, likewise for 2p coins; 5p coins in a quantity up to an amount of £5 and the same applies for 10p coins; 20p coins in a quantity up to an amount of £10, likewise for 50p coins; and £1 or £2 coins up to any amount. Limited-issue £5 and £20 coins are also legal tender up to any amount, although you'll very seldom encounter them among people's spending money, as they're mostly intended for collectors.

I checked with the Bank of England, and a spokesman said, with a chuckle, that legal tender rules barely applied to car boot sale transactions, but it is illuminating stuff to know anyway. Personally, I cannot see any circumstances in which I'd turn away handfuls of copper 'shrapnel' anyway, but I guess if some fashionista offers you a sack of 1p coins for a £20 designer jacket, you would be within your rights to turn her down...

Counterfeit notes

The good news is that much less than 1 per cent of all the English bank notes in circulation are fakes; in 2012, 719,000 examples were detected among the 3 billion out there in the wider economy. The most common forgery is the £20 note, not the £50 note as many think, and the introduction of new plastic notes from 2016 aims to cut forgeries even further.

The bad news is that you never quite know when one might pop up. Counterfeiters often target places where they can be confident that their forgeries won't be checked – a car boot being a prime example – and they have a habit of using large-denomination notes to pay for low-value items, robbing vendors of both 'genuine' change and their stock items.

The Bank of England, which issues all English banknotes, has plenty of advice for retailers so they can form a policy for staff to help them deal with forgeries. However, as a one-man band selling your own possessions, as you will be doing at a car boot, this is impractical. So the Bank instead urges you, as official advice, to...

'Remain vigilant at all times and check all banknotes being passed in a payment' (or, in my words: the onus is on you to ensure any banknotes you accept are legal)

There are various pieces of specialist equipment that can be used to spot counterfeits. These include an ultra-violet lamp to check in-built UV features in £5, £10, £20 and the latest £50 notes (featuring Messrs Boulton and Watt, rather than the Houblon of older examples), LED devices, and 'detector pens' that cause a chemical reaction between pen and paper. Chances are you won't possess any of these, and none of them are totally failsafe anyway.

Instead, the Bank has produced a leaflet entitled *Take a Closer Look* (available free by calling 020 7601 4878) with clear checking procedures. Its website also offers a 'virtual tour' of pukka notes, and there's a Banknote App available too. The Bank recommends you check several of the security features built into all banknotes for any you feel are suspect, which include:

- 'Bank of England' text on the front – you should be able to feel that this print is very slightly raised by running your finger across it.

- Watermark – when holding the note up to the light you should see an image of the Queen in the clear oval in the middle; '£20' and '£50' should also show up brightly in the watermark of the respective notes.

- Metallic thread – this is woven into every note, and shows up as silver dashes on the note surface (except on the latest £50 note, where it's fully embedded, with no dashes) and as a continuous dark line when held up to the light.

Take your time to closely examine two or more of these features on any high-value note handed over. Some people even use a small magnifying glass to do this. If you are suspicious any note offered to you is counterfeit, you are fully within your rights to refuse to take it, and to ask for alternative currency.

If you're unfortunate enough to be unwittingly passed a counterfeit note, then, sadly, the outlook isn't good.

It is totally worthless, and there is no chance that it can be replaced at a bank or Post Office for a genuine one. You would be committing an offence if you tried knowingly to use it for payment elsewhere, and many retailers have official policies in place where they will confiscate it and pass it on to the police for criminal analysis (genuine ones would be returned, though). Indeed, it is actually an offence to even retain a fake note; it must be passed to the police, who can add it to the database that helps them stamp out organised crime.

Be aware, though, that even tatty notes, if genuine, retain their face value. Banks will usually exchange a decrepit fiver or tenner for a crisp new one as long as there's a little over half of it left.

Counterfeit coins

Fake coins seem to be even more of a trader nemesis than notes. A 2013 survey found the level of pretend £1 coins had risen from 2.74 per cent to 3.04 per cent in a year, which is a serious cause for alarm at the Royal Mint, which regularly checks large caches of coins to weed out as many counterfeits as it can.

Most, although not all, forging seems to centre on the £1 coin, and they can be hard to spot. But the Mint has issued these guidelines to help you spot a duff quid:

- The milled edge is poorly defined and the lettering is uneven in depth and/or spacing, or is poorly formed.

- The designs are not sharp or well defined.

- The coin is unfeasibly shiny and golden; it shows little sign of age even though the date suggests it will have been in circulation for some time.

- The colour of the coin just doesn't look realistic – it doesn't match genuine coins.

Although the Royal Mint offers comprehensive printed and online information to make clear which designs and inscriptions correspond with specific dates, a busy car boot seller isn't going to have the time to check individual coins against such checklists. It will be much more a case of glancing at any £1 coins you're presented with, and handing back to the customer any that seem dodgy. They may look dismayed or bewildered. However, as said previously, suspicion of fakery is justification enough to reject it.

RECEIPTS

I've decided to lump the issue of receipts into this 'Problem' section because they are very rarely requested at boots, yet they are also prone to common misconceptions as to their legal status.

'Asking for a receipt' is one of those glib pieces of consumer advice that is next to useless, certainly in the context of amateur sellers at a car boot.

There is no legal requirement for a private seller to issue a receipt. It is a convention rather than a law. A buyer can request it but you don't have to provide one, and it follows that you do not need to provide your name and address.

As a private seller, though, you may feel you want to offer a receipt, perhaps for a larger and more expensive item. And some people may request one from you for their own business expenses, say in the case of a theatre set designer buying props for a production. If you're happy to write out details of the transaction along with a phrase like 'Paid with thanks' or 'Received with thanks', then fine, but you are under no obligation to divulge any personal details.

CHAPTER 10
Staying the course

It's not an easy job to forecast when precisely you are likely to be busy or slack. This will naturally depend on such factors as the weather, the size of the car boot sale and the sheer randomness of the flow of visitors.

In general, you will always be busy at the outset, with some sort of clamour as you open for trade, even if you've slightly delayed getting started so those pesky and intimidating early start hustlers (see Chapter 7) won't be in your face as you set up shop. There will then be a lull as the crowds start to pour in through the gate, but from then on the footfall is very unpredictable. Buyers can come in droves, waves or, seemingly, not at all.

On a sunny day, at a big boot close to any centre of dense population, you'll probably be amazed at the sheer number of browsers there are. But the crowds will always be thinner if it's a dull day, even if rain isn't forecast at all.

If you've set up at or before 7 a.m., the morning can seem like a long one when you look at your watch to discover that it's 'only' 9 a.m. For most morning events, which will tend to end any time between noon and 2 p.m., you're not even at the halfway point. Time to have a coffee, stamp those feet to keep warm – and buckle down.

KEEP THAT SALES PATTER GOING!

Even if you've had a blazing first two hours, and seem to have sold most of your really good stuff, don't let your resolve slip.

Buyers can pitch up at any time throughout the whole affair, while many people retrace their steps and comb back through all the stalls they've already given the once-over.

At about 10 a.m. you should consider a roughly mid-point reshuffle. With your clothes on sale, for instance, some rearranging and tidying might be needed to make the selection look tempting again. 'All my best stuff is at the front on my rails,' says Kerry Ball. 'If it all sells, then I do need to re-sort it and bring the next best items – or anything with the better labels – to the front. Keep shifting your best stuff forward to keep it moving.'

Another mid-period focus should be families.

You see plenty of family groups ambling their way round car boots, usually a mum with children in tow or in a pushchair, but frequently a couple with two or more children. To be frank, you can sometimes detect they are facing tough economic times, as the shopping is often for the basics or for clothes and toys that would be out of reach at new retail prices.

'The women are the ones who are doing the real looking,' says Kerry. 'Men generally have the children in tow, so they [the women] will be the ones rooting through your toy boxes.' As the remaining selling time dwindles, Kerry will often give away a small toy to such kids. This naturally goes down a treat with the parents, who then feel more inclined to take advantage of Kerry's generous bulk prices. Everyone wins.

From about 11 a.m. a mixture of returning browsers and a smattering of latecomer new ones will be beginning their perusal for end-of-day bargains.

You might also do well to pick that time to review the remains of your wares, and start to make a mental checklist about what items you'll be happy to take home to keep for another day or seek a different disposal route for, and which things you really want to see the back of and maybe – in some cases – would almost rather give away than have hanging around. Think of it as the tipping point between holding out for the best price and getting rid for the best outcome…clearing the decks.

In doing this, you mentally select the things on which you can now start to offer fantastic deals to the very next person whose interest is snagged by them. Engage the browser in a friendly way and say directly that you'd take an offer on a whole quantity of the same, and even name an irresistible price – 'The whole lot for a tenner', 'You can have the box-full for two quid', that kind of thing.

If there are several people milling around your pitch, rubbing their chins in uncertainty, it really helps to call out your clearance offers: 'Everything a pound or less', or 'Make me an offer', or 'I don't want to take any of this home', or even the classic BOGOF mantra: 'Buy one item and you can have a second one for free.' For those who are too polite to ask, this unlocks the negotiating gates and unleashes bargaining boldness. It won't do you any harm: in fact, quite the reverse. If you've been standing there all morning with the complete, huge but deeply unfashionable crockery service from your late Great Aunt Maureen's house, and you haven't had a bite, then it really is time to bail. What's worse: 'giving it away' for a fiver or having to schlep to the tip with it on your next day off?

No need to slash prices on your good stuff, of course – the things that you'll happily keep, perhaps try selling online, or maybe give to a friend or family member later. But even there you can begin to get extremely generous with, for example, pairs of jeans that haven't sold at £4, offered at £2, or £1 baby clothes now going at the rate of two for £1. It's money in the bank, less than you'd hoped for perhaps, but money nonetheless, and the items are off your plate.

Not only that, but if punters detect you're really keen to shift your leftovers, they may well buy rather more than they intended. Late morning is the time when many car boot buyers take stock, see how much spending money they have left, and start to amble about with a mission to use it if they possibly can. Make sure as much of this 'discretionary spend' comes your way – and not someone else's – as possible.

You might be surprised, as you engage in all this active marketing, that people around you don't seem to be following suit. I've noticed this myself on many occasions. A large proportion of car boot sellers seem to make absolutely no active effort to sell what they've brought.

Okay, so I acknowledge that I possibly have a restless nature where others don't. But if I'm doing a car boot, then I have a strictly limited window of opportunity. I can veg out afterwards but, while I'm there and the customers keep coming, I'm going to make hay with what little sunshine there is.

EARLY CLOSERS CAN BE LOSERS

Car boot sales have set opening and closing times, even if they aren't strongly enforced. We've talked in general throughout this book in terms of Sunday mornings, as this is by far the most popular time for them to be staged. But they also take place on Sunday afternoons, on Saturdays and in a few cases on weekdays. I am sure entrepreneurs would stage rolling, 24-hour, seven-day-a-week events if only local councils would grant permission (which they surely never will).

It is extremely annoying for buyers, who have paid to be there during the advertised opening hours, when sellers start to pack up before the official end time – sometimes well before, with an hour or more to go. I mean, you've paid your money to come in and, while you acknowledge that much of the good stuff is plundered early on, you do expect to be able to pick your way through everything else until the metaphorical bell goes.

To be at a boot that ends at 1 p.m. and to see tables being cleared at 11.30 a.m. and boxes being stuffed back into cars is absolutely exasperating.

Sellers, really, are missing a trick, because there are always buyers circling right until the very last moment. Many's the time I've offloaded goodly quantities of stuff just at the point when I reckoned I'd seen the last potential buyers some time previously. Not only that, but if you wait to pack up after the end time, you might just strike it lucky with a regular seller, who might make you an absolutely last-minute offer. Obviously, the price is never going to be big, but it is yet another opportunity to offload and turn even more unwanted clutter into cash.

DON'T BLOW IT ALL

As things are running down, it can be all too tempting to feel your takings burning a hole in your pocket. You've a good wedge of notes stashed away on your person and pockets bulging with coins, and there are a few things on other stalls nearby that have caught your eye. Now it's relatively quiet, you feel the pull to wander over and have a mooch around.

This is all very well, but keep a few things in mind:

- You've come here to get rid, so are you sure you want to start acquiring all over again?

- Those items on the stall next but one along certainly look like bargains, but are you just buying them because they are there, rather than because you really want them?

- You need all the money raised at the car boot sale today for a specific use or project, or maybe to chip away at a credit card bill or to pay off a debt, so are you letting your self-discipline slip by doling some of it out?

If you want to take that cash home, then avoid the temptation to buy elsewhere. And steer well clear of the hot-dog van, although you knew that already, didn't you?

'Stick to your guns, especially at the beginning,' advises car boot old hand Kerry Ball. 'If I'm selling, I'm there to sell and that is it. I don't look around at all, even though the temptation kills me, and especially if I've made quite a lot of money. If I'm there to sell, then that is my sole focus.'

CONGRATULATIONS – YOU'VE DONE IT!

At this stage, as the very last few possible buyers drift away, you should have managed two major achievements for all the time, effort and doggedness you've poured into this venture.

First, you should be almost uncomfortable with the money pressing at the seams of your pockets.

What would you call a good result?

I've asked all sort of friends, contacts and even strangers and it seems that the typical result, for a traditional boot fair to which they've taken a car packed full of mixed items, is usually between £80 and £125.

A few people I know have come away with much more, £300–400, and one or two – who I suspect had a passive attitude to selling, had very unappealing stock, or else spent their takings on other things – ended the day with £40–50.

I'd say that if you came away with £150, after paying the pitch fee of £10–15, then you could count yourself as having done very well. Not much for a city high-flyer but welcome extra money, cash in pocket, for most of us; £200 would be excellent.

Your second achievement? Well, you have successfully cleared your home of a large quantity of unwanted items, freeing up living space, and haven't added anything to Britain's landfill problem.

Not only that, but you've reconnected with the genuine market mentality. You might think it sounds far-fetched but I firmly believe you add genuine experience to your life skills after selling at a car boot sale. You have to spend time preparing, hone your display and presentation abilities, deal with all kinds of characters, market your goods with gusto, constantly adjust your prices and outlook, and use a variety of techniques to hit your goal while all the time being aware of threats and potential problems. If your day job doesn't involve selling or interfacing with the public, it's a steep learning curve, but if you've negotiated it well then you should feel justly proud of yourself.

IT'S TIME TO PACK UP AND GO HOME. PHEW!
The show's over and it's time to pack up the car and get out of there.

As you survey what's left of your wares, now is a good time to divide up what you'll keep and what you intend to get rid of. Separate the things out into dedicated containers while you have the chance, which will save time later.

I often see mixed job lots of miscellaneous items up for auction on eBay, usually touted as 'ideal for car booting' or somesuch. What this means, of course, is that it's actually the unsold residue from someone's car boot sale effort, and is precisely the opposite of that advertised – it's not ideal for a boot because it failed to sell the first time.

Nevertheless, many online chancers don't appreciate this, and if your start price is low enough – and there is a sizeable quantity – then you're almost bound to get a couple of them bidding to relieve you of it. And that's even if you stipulate 'Collection in person only'. Someone will think they can turn it into cash.

Alternatively, you can donate it to charity, although spare a thought for charity shop volunteer workers. They don't want to receive rubbish; they want items that they have a decent chance of selling to raise funds. If you genuinely feel that what didn't sell at the car boot is little more than trash, then you really need to take it down to the council dump where you can recycle whatever can be and dispose of the remainder properly.

If, though, you have the car boot bug, then you probably want to hang on to your unsold stuff for next time (see Chapter 11, coming up shortly).

THE SLOW GOODBYE

Any heavily attended happening these days, whether it's a concert at the 02 or a major county show, tends to need marshalling as everyone rushes for the exit when proceedings come to an end. Car boot sales also require a controlled finish, like most other large outdoor events.

If the venue is adjacent to a busy traffic thoroughfare, it will take a while to leave, so be prepared to be patient. It's amazing how agitated people can get when they have to queue to leave. Make sure you give yourself a twenty-minute gap between finally closing the car door and actually exiting the site, because the jam could be slow to clear. No need to get flustered; just think of the successful morning you've had and stay cool! When you finally get home, you'll be able to put your feet up and have a victory nap!

CHAPTER 11
Fancy doing it again?

There's little doubt that some people can become car boot sale obsessives, as much on the selling side as the buying one.

If your toe in the water has brought out a new set of skills in you, then you might be itching to have another go.

And why not, if you've plenty more stuff to sell, or you have a deceased relative's house to clear, or maybe have friends who'd like you to sell for them. If they're personal possessions and you're not doing it for a living, you are absolutely free to do so. Each year, Kerry Ball decides she's going to sell at three boots per season at a variety of local venues.

'After each of the first two, I carefully fold everything so they'll still be fresh and clean, ready for the next time, when I'll add them to any new stuff that comes my way,' she says. 'Anything left over at the end of the season goes straight to charity.'

Selling at a car boot takes a good deal of effort if it's going to work well, but if you've also enjoyed it, then you too can start doing more. If you don't feel you have enough of a car-load to make another one worthwhile, why not team up with friends or colleagues to share the experience and spread the pressure, and to make good use of your hard-won experience?

However, if you get too proficient, sell week in, week out, and start spending your profits to acquire stock that you can make a killing on, you'll need to read the next section.

CHAPTER 12
Are you, in fact, a trader?

When you become a regular car boot sale trader, then you will most likely cross the line between amateur seller and small businessman or woman.

And that may be just the thing for you, if you feel you have a flair for sourcing and selling items that people clamour for. It could be the making of you, maybe even setting you off along the road to vast riches and great personal success. After all, TV business guru Lord Alan Sugar is just one tycoon who started his empire by selling from the back of a van.

If you're canny, you will be buying your goods – maybe from auction websites, newspaper adverts, personal contacts or cash-and-carry outlets; perhaps they will actually be made by you, or even picked up in savvy bankrupt stock deals – and selling them on to the public at a roaring profit.

You might think the differentiation is blurred, or that you can operate below the parapet to rake in some sizeable chunks of extra income, but actually the law is pretty clear-cut about trader status.

You are a trader if:

- The goods you're offering were bought specifically for resale, and have never really been your 'personal property'.

- You sell at car boot sales on a very regular basis.

- You employ someone to help you sell.

- You sell similar items on street markets, from home or over the Internet.

- You earn a significant part of your income from selling at car boots.

In fact, there are no hard and fast rules. But you will probably be aware of what kind of seller you are anyway, and if two or more of the above apply to you, then you almost certainly are a trader.

At issue here are basic principles which have been put in place to protect consumers and safeguard tax revenue. And that is, that you can't pretend not to be a trader if you, in fact, are one.

Here are some pointers to help you start life as a legitimate trader.

WHO ARE YOU?

If you don't trade under your own name – even if you don't have limited company status – you are legally bound to show details of your name and address somewhere it can be clearly seen and if necessary noted down. And even if you do trade under your own name, you may need to display your contact information if the purchaser is likely to need that information to make a purchasing decision – such as, for example, knowing where to bring something to have it serviced or a warranty honoured.

IS YOUR STUFF MERCHANTABLE?

What you sell, as a trader, must be of the quality and condition you claim it to be, whether it's new or second-hand. Clearly, if you're selling antiques, there is some leeway here for the aesthetic appeal of something to be its selling point, rather than its practical use. But you are not allowed to pass off something with qualities that it turns out not to possess.

Your buyers have the right to a full refund if they find fault with the item immediately. But they are also entitled to a partial refund, proper repairs or full replacement for up to six months after purchase. After that time, customers can also claim one of these methods of redress if the item can be proven to have an intrinsic fault. Only if you pointed out such faults before the customer bought it are you free from these obligations. These are all part of consumers' statutory rights, which can't be compromised. Therefore, signs that state something like 'Sold as seen' or 'No refunds' are actually illegal.

Your goods need to be safe, and also to comply with relevant safety standards.

IS IT YOURS?

Handling stolen goods incurs even harsher punishment than stealing them, so make sure anything you buy to sell is legitimate. In your own interest, when buying goods, ask for a receipt and proper identification, and notify police if you discover something has been stolen. After all, you don't want someone else's shady reputation to taint your new good standing as a trader, do you?

ARE YOU FAIR?

If you trade unfairly in any way, you may be open to a civil prosecution if your customers turn out to be right to be disgruntled.

One area you are obliged to be fair about is pricing. Prices need to be clearly displayed on or next to your items, and can't be misleading in any way, especially in relation to hidden charges. Nonetheless, this need be no barrier to bargaining, so don't feel such a rule calls for a negotiating straitjacket.

INTENDING TO SELL FOOD?

Food's a tricky area, fraught with danger unless you adhere strictly to food safety, labelling and advertising rules laid down by the European Food Safety Authority. These regulations extend to being able to supply on-demand information about suppliers and ingredient sources. If you do sell food, you must be registered with the local Environmental Health Agency, and observe rigid hygiene standards. It's a highly regulated area, with stiff penalties for neglecting your responsibilities, but, if you can make it work, then good for you.

IS IT GENUINE?

Misleading descriptions are bad but selling copied, ripped-off, counterfeit or fake items is totally illegal for copyright and trademark reasons, and goods passed off as rivals' products are also forbidden. Any film/DVD you sell must have a British Board of Film Classification certificate, or you could face a massive fine and possible prison sentence.

For all of the above, you need to variously take heed of the Companies Act, the Consumer Protection Act, the Price Marking Order and the Consumer Protection from Unfair Trading Regulations Act – which is the replacement for the Trades Description Act – and maybe even the Food Safety Act. But don't worry: your local Trading Standards office can furnish you with copious amounts of useful trading information, and point you in the right direction where it can't help.

The regular patrols of car boot sales made by Trading Standards officers are incognito, and if you are a trader masquerading as an amateur seller then chances are they will soon be able to tell, and might well be on your case to make sure that you're operating within the law.

That's almost all the heavy stuff to do with trading. Apart from the money.

Life as a trader will inevitably mean that the money you make forms part of your income. And it goes without saying that you must keep detailed records for your annual accounts, from which your income tax will be calculated.

Part Two
Buying at Car Boot Sales

CHAPTER 13
Why a car boot?

Sunday morning in Britain is a tale of two countries. For many – maybe the majority – it's a time of relaxation, recharging and recovery. It's the one truly restful day of the week, when the alarm doesn't need to be set and the work agenda is on hold. It's also the morning after the night before, when the effects of alcohol, eating out, a gig or concert, partying, or even just a late night watching movies or playing computer games can be peacefully slept off.

Being up before dawn, with the air anything from chilly to downright freezing, and heading off to a dew-soaked field to rifle through other people's possessions will be anathema to these slumbering masses.

GET-UP-AND-GO TYPES

Yet the yin to this yang is the car booter. And this type of Brit is hardly of the singular weirdo type. Hundreds and hundreds of thousands of people are up and out as first light is breaking. And what's more, for many it's an addiction like running or swimming – something from which they feel vague withdrawal symptoms if they can't get their 'fix' often enough.

The lure of the car boot for buyers is the tantalising pull of the unknowable and the huge potential opportunities of largely unstructured human interaction. Whatever it is you're looking for, it might just be there this time, and if it isn't then something else is going to leap out at you. Whatever the case, your expectation is that it's going to cost you peanuts, and you'll be returning laden with the kinds of bargains that no amount of discounting will ever yield in the conventional retail world.

WHAT MOTIVATES A CAR BOOT SALE BUYER?

The car boot sale buyer, once the browsing habit is established, rarely stops to question his or her motives. It's just the thing they do on a Sunday morning, an established norm. But here we can look at a few of the reasons why you might choose to start visiting car boot sales.

Financially stretched

We've all been enduring the longest recession in living memory. While interest rates are low, other living costs have been rising relentlessly, and this is all set against a backdrop of job insecurity, stagnant wages and unemployment itself. What's more, even graduates are emerging into a world of work where good jobs are often impossible to come by and employers are offering internships and zero-hours' contracts as take-it-or-leave-it conditions.

Basically, times are tough and disposable income scarce for a wide range of working people.

Car boot sales, from the smallest to the most enormous, are packed with opportunities to get what you want for a fraction of what it will cost you in the shops. The vast majority of the goods on offer are, of course, ahem, 'pre-loved' – in the real world, second-hand – but that is not to say an item of clothing, a DVD, a key piece of kitchenware or big-brand toy won't be perfectly all right. What's more, you'll be able to inspect it and, if there are flaws, negotiate hard. Try doing that in Debenhams!

If you know what you need, and are prepared to spend the time searching, car boot sales can save you an absolute fortune on items that your financial situation might otherwise deny you.

Special interest
If you're mad on gardening, DIY, cooking, reading, music, sport or whatever, and you really want to make the most of your hobby, car boots can be brilliant at furnishing you with the material and/or equipment you need at truly bargain prices.

Let's say your passion is cooking and you fancy expanding your horizons away from British food and into, say, Middle Eastern flavours. Buying a tajine pot might cost you a fortune from a cookware shop, only for you to find that you don't really like it. Picking one up that's an unwanted, barely used wedding present for a couple of quid means you can experiment with it and know you haven't wasted money.

Fancy having a shot at golf but don't want to spend thousands on all the kit only to find that it's simply a great way to spoil a good walk, as the old joke goes? Pick up your clubs, bag, trolley, balls, spikes and Pringle (style) jumper at a car boot and you'll have all the gear, even if you have no idea. If you really like Sundays out on the links, you can upgrade once you've got a handle on your handicap.

If you do a bit of weekend DJ-ing and look for rare dance-floor fillers, you can take a risk on a handful of offbeat LPs for mere pennies and know that you haven't lined iTunes' coffers for tracks that don't rock the house.

Whatever it is you need for your passion in life, a car boot sale will eventually yield it, probably saving you from vast expense.

Fashion magpie

You know the brands you like, the ones that fit you perfectly or the labels you aspire to, but you simply can't afford their high-street prices.

Car boot sales can be a shortcut to getting the look you want, with unwanted examples of all the top names waiting to be found among the (doubtless) large number of garments that definitely aren't your size, style or make. A weather eye out for the good stuff will, sooner or later, get you what you want, for precious little outlay. And you might, just might, chance upon a couture gem that has somehow slipped through everyone's fashion filter until you lucked out. That happens more often than you might imagine.

It's the same for shoes, hats, accessories, unopened cosmetics, haircare items; with a core constituent of sellers being women, every car boot becomes a veritable fashion fair…mixed in with a sizeable element of jumble sale. You will be your own cut-price style editor, and no one need ever know your source, unless you choose to tell them.

Kids' stuff

Children are fickle, and they just will keep on growing. This does tend to set their consumption of toys, books, clothes and shoes at a different pace to adults. Luckily, at car boot sales a large number of the vendors are parents anxious to recoup at least some of the expense of children's paraphernalia, and just dying to pass it on to other mums and dads who can find value in it.

The boot is a great source of abandoned hobby stuff, from art materials and garden playthings to games consoles and dressing-up clothes. So if your children have current passions that you think might one day flicker into disinterest, then this is the best place to stock up without spending a fortune.

Crafts

Making and mending, sewing and stitching, sanding and nailing, painting and decorating; in fact, for just about any craft-based activity you can name you will find a ready source of materials, tools and accessories at a car boot sale. And, as for fabric, you'll most likely find the raw material as well as garments that can be cut or converted. The trained eye can alight upon wool, thread, buttons, ribbon, buckles and more that's crying out for dexterous new hands, and is going for a song.

Home improvement

If you're intending to turn your humble abode into a palace, car boot sales are usually great sources of items that can add to the transformation.

From something as simple as a three-quarters-full tin of paint to large items of furniture, and everything in between, the car boot is a home-improver's goldmine where you might be able, for instance, to pick up new door furniture that transforms your house's original décor, or more pleasing storage jars that add a homely touch to the kitchen, or that small box of tiles to complete a bathroom transformation; and, indeed, a tile cutter to make them fit, and the three-quarters of a tube of the right grouting for a few pence, which means the job can be finished off for almost nothing.

Garden & garage

Weekend visits to garden centres or car-accessory shops can be expensive outings, where you are a captive audience for these thriving leisure industries. But at car boots, you'll find a vast array of garden-related items and products – from the humblest packet of seeds to the biggest lawnmowers – and there's usually a large choice of products and accessories for your car, some of it used and/or opened, but a lot of it brand new: tools, oils, spares and duplicates from cars that got sold or scrapped before the owner had the chance to lavish any care on them.

Collector

Whether it's rare books, antique china, vintage toys, things shaped like frogs or brass ornaments, you name it, a car boot sale is a great hunting ground.

Of course, the events are random in their nature and unpredictable in what they throw up. As an experienced collector, you might find that many visits fail to turn up what you're looking for, but, then, wham! When you do alight upon a rare item that's going to be a fantastic addition to your collection – and possibly quite valuable in itself – the feeling of elation is like no other.

Feel the need to start a collection but not sure what to go for? A few car boot trips and you're bound to see something that fires your imagination. And once you're off, you're sure to be hooked.

Small business, trader or dealer

If you know exactly what you're chasing for your small business, a car boot sale may well be a weekly destination that pays out time after time.

This could be something as simple as buying your office stationery in cheap job lots, or tools for your trade.

More likely is that you deal in antiques, collectibles, jewellery or art and have long recognised that car boots are crammed with people who sometimes don't know what they're selling, and among whose items are likely to be the things you know have real value.

If you're this kind of buyer, then you'll have a keen and practised eye, and you won't be distracted by anything that isn't core to what you trade in. You'll spot gems at fifty paces and your car boot trips will have been honed over years of searching...and plentiful great finds.

Don't know what I'm looking for...

You may feel you fit into none of the above categories, or else a niche area I haven't defined. That's fine. That's actually normal. The vast majority of car boot sale visitors on the buying side turn up with a completely open mind. They don't quite know what they want, but they're getting a great kick out of scanning and searching and, they hope, alighting on something either unexpected or else long desired. The process is inexact, the spread of items for sale chaotic, but it's totally absorbing, and therein lies the appeal.

You either do or you don't quite know what you want, but who knows what you will find? You can take a specific mission and a 'wants' list with you. But don't expect to be able to tick everything off. It depends entirely on what's there on the day, and your buying strategy may well be swayed simply by what you come across on your search.

I fully anticipate you may have read this section and scoffed. You go to car boot sales for entirely different buying reasons, known only to yourself. But I'll wager the impetus is much the same as everyone else's: to nose your way through the rough to find that diamond, whatever it might be, and then to secure it for a bargain price. As I said at the start of the book, these are the least restricted, most open, most freely negotiable markets in the country – with everything at them to play for.

CHAPTER 14
Choosing a car boot

The last section, I trust, confirmed that you'd be interested – at the very least – in seeing what a car boot sale is like if you've never been to one before, even if you may still have residual reservations about the event itself and whether you're going to 'enjoy' it. I mean, if you are fiercely anti-shopping, and don't like mingling with all and sundry of a Sunday morning, then it's probably not for you. Similarly, some people have a bit of a thing about second-hand goods that sends a shudder of revulsion through them at the very thought. If that's you, and you only feel secure in Ikea or John Lewis, or uncomfortable about handling anything that hasn't been packed in a clinical environment and hermetically sealed, then you might also want to avoid bootys altogether.

Recognising the sort of buyer you are will have an influence on the type of car boot sale you gravitate towards.

In my experience, there are several key types, and they project very different atmospheres. More on this shortly. But before we look at that, clearly most of us are going to go to our nearest one, for obvious reasons of convenience and best use of our precious weekend time.

HOW TO FIND YOUR CAR BOOT SALE

There is no nationwide federation of car boot sale organisers, but there are some websites that claim to be nationwide
directories (see Appendix for details). By their nature, these
are not always up to date, as events are often staged by
individuals and can be prone to cancellation or, sometimes,
abandonment. On more than one occasion I've turned up
at a silent field or padlocked car park to find that the event
isn't actually on, or no longer exists, and this has generally
been down to redundant information that should have
been deleted from a site. Extremely frustrating.

In trying to find a local event that you think will be enjoyable, it's usually a good idea to type your home town or
area and then 'car boot sale' into a search engine and see
what comes up.

As old events close and new ones open constantly, it's
impossible to put a precise figure on the number of car
boots staged across the country. It may be as many as 2,000.
At the time of writing, a quick look at carbootjunction.com
revealed there were 1,751 events listed in its database directory, which gives a reasonable idea of the scope of 'the
hobby'.

In my experience of recent years, even quite small sales tend
to have their own website, often an extremely simple one,
and you can quickly and easily tell that the event is still live
from the most recent update or posting about the upcoming date. Just as many, and increasingly more, will have a
presence on social media networks like Facebook and
Twitter. In addition, most of them will include a phone

number for an organiser, which will take you either straight to that person or to up-to-date recorded information about the status of the boot fair.

The other, very reliable source of information about upcoming boots is to be found in your local paper. If an advert has had to be paid for, you can bet your bottom dollar the organiser is going to go ahead with it, come what may. The ads are often tiny, and squeezed into slots at the edges of pages, but search your local *Chronicle* or *Courier*, *Times*, *Telegraph* or *Mercury* and you'll find them.

With the emergence of the 'indoor car boot sale' or the 'table boot fair', and variations thereof, as the modern-day successors to jumble sales, these smaller and more parochial events tend to be promoted in newsagents' and Post Office windows, on supermarket free pinboards, parish notice boards and magazines/newsletters, in church halls, schools and community centres, and sometimes by the reliable method of pinning a flyer, encased in waterproof plastic, to lamp posts and telegraph poles. These happenings are not always held during the key car boot slot of Sunday morning, and so give you extra bonus events to go to that could yield just what you're looking for.

And if you're totally new to the car boot phenomenon, or have recently moved into a new area, you can always ask friends, neighbours, fellow students or work colleagues. If you're worried about what people think, then seek out a kindred spirit who you know isn't going to judge you for your desire to go weekend bargain-hunting. I say this because I know, even among my own wide circle of friends, there are plenty who would recoil at the very thought. With some mates, I might not even care to mention the subject. It doesn't mean I value them less as friends, or worry that they'll give me a ribbing; it's just that it is my bag and it isn't theirs, and that's fair enough (although, obviously, I really think they don't know what they're missing!).

AS GOOD AS IT SAYS?

Of course, any events you see promoted and advertised either online or on good old pieces of paper can purport to be one thing and turn out to be another entirely. Terms like 'old established', 'popular' and 'famous' are meaningless, and don't necessarily mean that the pickings will be good, or the number of pitches numerous.

When a promoter says the car boot is 'huge' or 'massive' then you can assume that it will at least be big enough to be worth your while. Even then, they're totally reliant on who turns up on the day. If you can spend the time researching some actual online reviews, or talking to people who've been to the event in question, you'll get a much clearer idea of the scale and whether it's consistently colossal or can tend towards the thin and meagre.

In my time, I've been to every type, size and location of boot fair, and I trust sharing this experience will help.

Sunday market/inner city

In my time living in London, I used to go to the Sunday New Covent Garden Market that made full use of the empty concrete expanse vacated by the fruit and veg whole-salers over the weekend. There are other similar events staged in the middle of big cities across the nation. A huge constituent here were produce sellers, with quite a few butchers and cut-price grocery sellers lumped in too, but there was plenty of space for sundry traders of cheap new clothes or second-hand tat, and a few private sellers, to make up the numbers. It could occasionally throw up a bargain, but more generally reflected the poverty of the surrounding social housing.

Suburban sprawl

These are my favourite kinds of car boots. They're usually held on the fringes of towns and cities at the juncture where a combination of leafy suburbs and high-density housing estates give way to semi-rural countryside, which means that, occasionally, enormous fields can accommodate a huge number of sellers.

The reason I like them is that you get a rich mixture of vendors. You have the affluent middle classes, you have the hard-pressed working classes, you get students and kindly old couples, mother-and-daughters, you have the hardened traders – ranging from virtual rag-and-bone men to quasi-respectable antique specialists – the blokes selling tools and trade gear, and every other type of seller in between. The mix is marvellously random.

You also have quite a few of what I call 'trade moonlighters'. This might be typified by a self-employed removals person, a builder, roofer or a courier. The key is that people like these have a large empty van or pick-up at their disposal over the weekend, and their jobs often mean they come across stuff that's going begging, can be had for nothing, and can be sold to make some useful extra cash in hand. A removals man, for example, might be asked to dispose of household items one of his clients needs to get rid of; a roofer might have a loft to clear at the same time as replacing rafters, insulation and tiles; and a builder will often have the chance to clear all kinds of stuff out of skips.

What I like is that they generally just tip their stock out on to grass or a tarpaulin and let the public do the searching and sifting. They usually don't quite know what's there and so the opportunity for bargains is strong.

Yet even if raking through old junk isn't really your scene, these town-and-country bazaars are sure to offer the most choice of every type of item.

Small, local, country

These probably make up the biggest single group of car boot sales. You might expect to find anything from about 80 to more than 250 pitches to browse in locations which are often, if you'll forgive the mild insult to otherwise pleasant localities, in the middle of bloody nowhere.

These boots, I find, tend to have a lower proportion of traders and a higher number of amateurs, and they generally feel less ruthlessly commercial than their more urban counterparts. Their small scale is reflected, obviously, in the relatively limited pickings, but in my experience, if you go regularly then it won't be long before you scratch up something fantastic.

Small, local, 'schools 'n' churches'

These boots tend to be organised by volunteers as semi-regular or occasional fundraisers for a specific cause, like a parent-teacher association in a school or a revenue-generating committee for a church or village hall.

Their scope is usually limited by the available space, as they are most likely held in a car park or other hardstanding, rather than in a field.

The small scale is both the best and the worst thing about them. The hard-nosed car boot 'pros' probably won't bother, meaning the attendance will be smaller and more courtly, and so the chances of picking up something sweet are higher. The downside, though, is that there won't be a tremendous amount to go at.

Boots like this will have a larger proportion of toys and children's clothes, so if that's what you need, then don't dismiss them. Plus, you might be able to fit one in on the way back from a bigger event, making it something of a bonus.

Posh area, posh stuff?

If you pick a boot sale in an expensive area, will it offer the most bargains? That would certainly be logical. Just as for charity shops in smart towns, the quality of items on offer is likely to be better than average…and rich people do have a tendency to 'get rid' sooner than the rest of us, who will 'make do' for rather longer, especially with upmarket labels and brands.

But experienced buyers already compute this, and know there will be fierce competition. As long as you aren't specifically chasing Dolce & Gabbana, Apple, Jimmy Choo and Nike, car boots in less upmarket areas could be just as productive, even if the goodies don't come to hand so readily. A bargain-hunting mentality can be counter-intuitive, so don't be too ready to dismiss an event until you've tried it a few times and got the measure of the thing.

How much will it cost you?
You would expect to pay for a selling pitch at a boot, and you'd be right. But what about as a buyer?

Well, a good number of events do make a small charge for entry, although there is no set pattern. One-man-band organisers presumably need every penny, while the people who stage the really large ones know that there will be so much to go for that the public won't resent coughing up a small amount to get in.

Different events have different ways of charging. Some demand a charge per car before you park, no matter how many people are on board, and this is usually either £1 or £2. Others let you park for free and then levy an entry charge per person at the pedestrian gate. This can be 20p, 50p or maybe even £1. The organiser has to weigh up the costs of stationing people to perform these charging duties against the returns, but at a really large car boot clearly the sum raised is significant extra income for the landowner or 'impresario', while a relatively unimportant amount for each individual visitor.

On the other hand, I know of several excellent boots where no charge for parking or entry is made…and yet more where the turnstile is so poorly run – old man on an upturned milk crate, rusty tin for coins – that it's easy to stride right in without so much as dipping your hand in your pocket! Not, I hasten to add, that I am condoning gatecrashing…

CHAPTER 15

Getting going, getting ready, getting there

For the past several years I've been going car booting with a good friend who shares the same passion. We met as dads whose sons were in the same class at school, and once he'd let the cat out of the bag about his booting forays, we got on like a house on fire.

Anyway, one of the best things about having a partner to go with is that, once you've committed to that 6 a.m. start, you've got to do it. There can be no rolling over, flicking the alarm off and deciding to give it a miss! Or looking out of the window, seeing an overcast sky and deciding not to bother.

Because, of course, it can be quite a wrench to leave the comfort of your duvet on a cold morning. However, you will only be doing so following frequent checks the day before on the most crucial deciding factor on whether to go to a boot or not...

THE WEATHER!

The British weather is the deal-breaking 'X' factor of the car boot sale.

In times long gone, the threat of heavy rain or storm-force gales the day before would have been the instant decider, because there would often be no way of knowing whether the event had been cancelled at the last-minute, and turning up at a desolate, water-logged field would thus be avoided.

Thankfully, as mentioned previously, there are very few events these days that don't have their own website or online presence, however small, on social media. The combination of this easy access and accompanying instant updates means real-time information is almost always available – yet another reason to be pathetically grateful to the Web. You can log on, quickly find that Old Bob has cancelled because his lower field is under 3ft of floodwater, and find an alterative boot, or do something else that Sunday.

Some really determined event organisers will only ever cancel if the outlook is positively torrential. The show must go on.

But there is almost nothing less enjoyable than a car boot sale when it's chucking it down.

The key problem is that only the wiriest traders and most hardy private sellers will turn up. So it can turn out to be a colossal waste of time for all involved.

The night before, check the weather forecast either online, on TV or on the radio. When you see what's predicted, make up your mind.

Snow
It would be amazing if the event went ahead under a white-out, and if it did people would rightly and sensibly stay away.

Heavy persistent rain and high winds
Don't bother; you'll get soaked and the seller turnout will probably be poor.

Rain, standard British
If it's light, you could chance it, but many private sellers will be deterred, and if you're going to look for clothes or books then the results might be messy.

Drizzly
Borderline. It can drizzle for hour after hour in Britain but still be bearable if the temperature isn't too shivery. Quite a few of the heartier sellers will decide to give it a go, and so chances are there will be enough laid out for you to make the morning worthwhile.

Cloudy
All right. In fact, for me, cloudy or overcast is absolutely ideal for booting. The event won't be mobbed, because a large stratum of British society are short on motivation and cower from the risk of rain as much as the guarantee of it; plus, the sellers might be a bit shivery and therefore good targets for some take-no-prisoners bargaining.

'Sunny intervals'

Perfect boot weather for buyers. It only there were more days like these.

Very sunny/hot

Good for a day out, although concentrated browsing under a baking sun, with lots of kneeling down and bending over, might not suit everyone. And direct sunlight bouncing from a propped-up bedroom mirror or chrome kitchen gadget and inadvertantly blazing into your retina is a particularly uncomfortable experience.

I've also been at car boots when there's been an unexpected shower or hail storm. Not much can be done about that, but it didn't put me off personally even if all around me were grumbling and cursing. Our climate is, by its nature, unpredictable. So, no matter what is forecast, you'll want to carefully consider what you wear.

BE PREPARED

Footwear

Many car boot sales are held on grass fields, and the condition of the ground will vary depending on the time of year and recent levels of rainfall. Wellington boots will cover you in all eventualities, although they are not really too comfortable for lots of walking. Waterproof walking boots or shoes are a much better idea, as they're designed for tough terrain and they keep you dry.

If you know the ground is going to be largely dry, most kinds of trainers or normal outdoor shoes should be okay. But my recommendation, even in the hottest of summer heatwaves, would not be to wear sandals, pumps, espadrilles or flip-flops. The pitches are not uniform and sellers often have sharp or metallic objects on the floor or in front of their tables. There is a real risk that you might sustain a cut or stub a toe. Or, indeed, that someone else in the massed hordes of browsers will step on your foot by accident.

I've seen quite a few no-doubt otherwise sensible ladies striding around car boot sales in high heels or platform mules. I've never understood why. If that's you, then I sincerely hope you don't fall over, and suggest that you might like to rethink.

Clothing

You'll know what you are comfortable in. But, believe me, when it's really cold and you're slowly making your way around a big boot fair, you'll wish you'd worn your thermal long johns and vest, if you haven't done so.

Cargo trousers or shorts with various pockets are, obviously, very useful. Especially pockets that close with a zip or Velcro, so you know that your money, wallet, phone, keys and other personal essentials are safe. This isn't just to guard against pickpockets – although these scummy people do lurk around some boot fairs looking for other people's carelessness to take advantage of – but also to make sure…

⚑You don't drop anything⚑

If any of your valuables slip out of a pocket on to the ground, the chances of finding it again will be remote. So keep anything like that well secured. Also, you might consider leaving anything valuable but unnecessary to your day out at home, so that things like rings, bracelets, necklaces and expensive watches can't be mislaid.

Jeans are a good idea, actually, as their pockets are generally figure hugging yet commodious. The only downside is that when they get wet, they don't dry off easily.

As to your upper body, in winter you'll want to keep warm but not overheat, and in summer stay cool and unflustered but not suddenly feel cold. Like everything to do with the British weather, it's a tricky call.

I've worn an anorak when it looked like it might rain and then felt unbearably hot by mid-morning when the downpour threat had lifted. Other times, I've gone in a T-shirt and got a horribly burnt neck by midday, which made for a somewhat uncomfortable week at work afterwards.

You're probably old and wise enough to know what you should wear for a whole morning outside in the British climate. But I've come to the time-worn conclusion that the optimum combination is a light shirt, which means my neck won't get scorched, worn with a zip-up tracksuit top that's wind-cheating when done up and light when unzipped, and also has a couple of zip-up side pockets into which my small personal items – not least of which, my spending money – can be safely stowed. Plus a baseball cap to either keep the sun out of my eyes or the drizzle off my specs. I'd avoid a fleece, as it's potentially too sweaty, and a hoodie, as it's not even remotely wind- or waterproof. I'm no beacon of sartorial elegance at a boot, and I really don't care!

Backpack essential...

It depends on what it is you're searching for, of course, but a lightweight backpack is essential to booting. It can swallow many small and medium items, and leaves you hands-free.

...But what about other bags?

In the past I have taken a few carrier bags with me, in case I see something too bulky to sling over my shoulder, and still have to lug it round. To be frank, this was a waste of time, and I generally ended up taking them home still folded up. Almost everyone selling at a car boot has brought along a supply of old carrier bags of various different types, and if they're selling anything brittle or delicate – such as china, glass or artwork – then chances are they're going to have plenty of padding or protective material, such as old newspaper and bubblewrap, they will be happy to give you gratis.

Getting 'trolley-ed'

For years I disdained the idea of having something in which to transport my finds around. Then I started to realise that keeping going often got to be hard work towards the end of a really massive boot fair, so weighed down would I gradually become with bargains and impulse buys. It wasn't that I was spending more; I was just getting bolder and more skilled at striking while the iron was hot.

So, finally, I paid a fiver for a reasonable quality (second-hand!) shopping trolley, a lightweight one made from weatherproof plastic with a drawstring to seal up the top, pockets on the side, and sturdy wheels. It's not tartan, there's nothing chic about it, and it only comes out for boot fairs.

However... I have to say that it has transformed booting and massively eased the strain of lugging my plunder around a large field. I thoroughly recommend one if what you're looking for is likely to be heavy or, as I said, you begin to shop with gusto and want as much flexibility as possible. Your energy for searching and bargaining won't be sapped by the mere donkey work of carting everything around. Make sure any shopping trolley you do buy for booting is tough; the made-in-China cheapies don't look like they'd withstand uneven ground very well.

Plenty of regular booters have them, but I've also seen really robust four-wheeled hardcarts in circulation, as well as barrows, warehouse trolleys and even baby buggies being used as shopping carts. They really can make a big boot fair much easier on the back and lungs.

Just remember to keep them within sight at all times when you stop to browse. If your cart or wagon is open-topped, take a blanket or cover to conceal what you've bought as you make your rounds, in case someone is tempted to pilfer from you.

YOUR ESSENTIAL KIT

Mobile phone: make sure it's fully charged and, ideally, in a case so it won't get damaged if dropped. You may want to compare things online, to quickly research original prices or compatibility, look up potential values or identifying marks, words or brands... or, of course, check whether the person you're just about to buy for gives you the eager go-ahead or stops you from making a major purchasing blunder. My personal feeling, however, would be that a tablet computer like an iPad wouldn't be the thing to take – too bulky and open to loss or theft. Call me old fashioned, if you like.

Batteries: if you're on the hunt for gadgets that rely on battery power, make sure you have a set of the right batteries on full charge with you, so you can test any potential purchase on the spot. You might want to do the same with, say, bulbs or any other consumable parts essential to making the thing work.

Screwdriver, spanner, pliers or Allen key: once again, these could be essential to making a thorough working examination before buying, but ask the vendor first if they mind you probing for functionality, otherwise an argument could erupt.

Magnet: could be useful if you're looking at something metal but rusty.

Tape measure: this is an absolute must if you're buying things for the home that need to fit certain dimensions. Remember to have a list of possible lengths, depths, widths and heights to hand, too.

Protective gloves: necessary if you intend to look through old tools where sharp edges and points might be hard to spot

'The original': If you're searching for a replacement part, component or section, and it's easily portable, then remember to take the redundant one with you, as a pattern. You'll kick yourself if you buy the wrong-size thing by mistake.

Paper and pen: many of us can make a note on our phones, or text a message back to base, but if you don't have a mobile, or if it doesn't have that feature, make sure you have some way of making a note, taking an address or writing yourself a memo.

REFRESHMENTS

To be brutally honest, I have never had a decent cup of coffee at a car boot sale. It's always poor quality instant, hugely overpriced. And I try to avoid the attendant burger vans – partly because the fare looks unappetising and greasy, and partly, once again, because of the dreadful ratio of quality-to-value.

On the other hand, a flask of coffee or tea can be a mixed blessing if it isn't absolutely watertight. Too often it will spring a leak in my bag and wreck something I've just been delighted to buy, like a rare book.

My advice would be, have a decent beverage before you go, and another when you get back, but try to get round the boot fair 'dry'. If you really think you'll need refreshment, a small bottle of water is probably the best thing…and bought from a supermarket for a few pence rather than the £1.50 that you'll get charged on the day.

And for snacks? Well, anything that can go in your pocket, won't melt, and which can give you that vital energy burst when you feel like you can't go on but there are still another seven rows of stalls to rake through. A pre-bought cereal bar or some biscuits should do the trick and be good insurance against the munchies.

CASH, MOOLAH, SPONDULICKS, WEDGE, GREENBACKS, READIES...

It's one of the most vexing issues about going car booting as a buyer: how much money to take? Call it what you will, you'll need to take enough of it.

Few of us, of course, have an unlimited budget, and it would be blindingly obvious to suggest you take what you can afford to spend. But if you have a little financial flexibility, how do you estimate what you might need with you?

One method could be to think about what it is you are hunting, how much you expect to pay per item, and how many of those items you could feasibly carry. So, for example, if you collect teapots and you make it a rule never to spend more than a fiver on any one addition to your miniature museum, you know that you could probably manage to carry ten of them, so you might choose to take £50. Or if you need five pairs of trousers and five T-shirts, which would be quite a haul for most people, and you're not intending to spend more than £3 on any one garment, then you'll need a minimum of £30 on you.

Most of us browsers probably aren't quite sure what we might find, or indeed what we might buy, so we need to pick a figure. In my personal experience, I rarely spend more than £25–30 but will opt to take £50–60 just in case I strike gold in some way. I know that other people just take their allotted pocket money, like a gambler entering a casino with all the cash he's prepared to lose, and once they've reached the self-imposed limit, then that's it. And a very sensible approach that is, too.

Coining it

Having the right denomination on you is quite important. These events are fuelled by £1 and £2 coins, 50p, 20p and 10p pieces, and £5 notes. And these are the pieces of currency you need. Ten-pound notes are okay too, but when it comes to £20, and especially £50 notes, sellers have a right to be suspicious and may well be reluctant to take them from you if they feel your payment may turn out to be counterfeit. Small-value copper? By all means take it along – it's all money, after all.

Be very, very careful about revealing that you have any substantial amounts of cash on you. You simply never know who might clock your roll of notes as you search through your pocket or wallet, and you don't ever want to give scheming pickpockets the incentive to target you.

Very few sellers would countenance taking a cheque from a stranger, so it would be a pointless exercise taking your chequebook with you unless you were going to collect the item from the seller later. This would be an unusual transaction, and something you should probably steer clear of.

GETTING THERE: THE CAR IS KING

In order to be on a grand scale, boot fairs often take place in places that are off the beaten track and are hard to get to any other way than by car. One I go to regularly is held on a huge scrubby field underneath some electricity pylons at the junction between a motorway and a major A-road. It is just about possible to get there on foot, but it's pretty dangerous along rough-edged hard shoulders with cars and trucks thundering past just a few feet away; watching buyers struggle home along these unforgiving thoroughfares, weighed down with bags and boxes – or, on one occasion, balancing a television on one shoulder – gives me nightmares.

Closer to towns, it might be easy to get to the site on a bus, or maybe by walking from a railway station, but the legwork is rarely what can be termed a 'short hop'. Even if public transport is a feasible travel option, remember that you might not quite know in advance what you'll buy, and then you'll need to struggle home with it one way or another. How glad will you be taking your fishing rod or garden tools back on the No. 94? I went to one event and bought a large vintage steel advertising sign with particularly sharp, rusty corners, and then made my way home on a series of packed London Underground tube trains…petrified that some child would be thrown against its jagged extremities if the train lurched to a sudden halt. It was a hair-raising hour I don't care to repeat. Another time, I lugged a vintage Anglepoise lamp home on an overground train to discover that it was one of the most unwieldy objects it has ever been my misfortune to carry on public transport. Fortunately, it only cost me a pound, but it was a hellish journey

So, for the vast majority, and to preserve your sanity, going by car is the best and only method. And if you don't have one, or access to one, then you are at a serious disadvantage.

Parking is usually plentiful, and there are generally hi-vis jacketed marshals to organise proceedings. Still, bear in mind that you'll almost always be asked to park on grass and that it could be wet and/or muddy, sometimes excessively so. The chances of getting your car actually stuck in boggy ground will be very slight – the marshals will steer you away from anything too swampy – but if it's looking mildly treacherous just remember to stay calm and proceed slowly, in a low gear.

Buyers tend to arrive at car boots in a steady stream, but then everyone seems to want to leave at the same time in a mass exodus. Queuing to get out seems to be an unavoidable consequence of it being a successful or worthwhile event, but I am still amazed at how impatient people can be – at the lack of courtesy, the angry revving of engines, spinning tyres and general air of uncontained, aggressive frustration. Half the time, these folk seem to take their lack of restraint out on their own cars, which is exceedingly pointless.

Reckon on it taking ten to twenty minutes to leave the site and rejoin the road network. Maybe this is the time to have a drink or chat and, if you're in a pleasant part of the world, savour the scenery and, naturally, reflect on the great finds you've just made.

At the start of this chapter, I mentioned having a car boot buddy to enjoy the morning with. If you do have a friend who feels just like you, then make the effort to coordinate the organisation and go together. It's just a lot more fun that way, and you'll have someone to give you a second opinion on potential purchases, or stop you from paying too much or buying a turkey. Plus, of course, a kindred spirit to share the excitement and elation of great finds with. With my friend, we usually meet up halfway through the morning to compare finds; and when he comes across a cheap gem, I'm almost as pleased as he is that at least one of us has nabbed it. This is also a great opportunity to lead each other back to items we think the other might fancy. I've picked up several great things – that I somehow missed – like that.

CHAPTER 16

Your browsing strategy

Arriving at any car boot sale presents you with an immediate and pressing problem: just how are you going to tackle the vista of opportunity that has been laid out before you?

If you are a laid-back character with no particular agenda in mind and an indeterminate amount of time to devote to your bargain hunting, then you might be the sort of person who just wanders around with no particular route in mind. You'll amble from one stall to another in no special order, much like a bumblebee might dart at random from one flower to the next, lured to the following stall by bright shiny things that sort of beckon you over.

I have to say straight off, that wouldn't be me.

I've got a limited amount of time and, in general, an awful lot of stuff to look at, and I need to have a strategy worked out in advance so I can cover everything and then still have enough time left over to, for example, retrace my steps, or return to reconsider something I've mentally bookmarked.

I like to extract the first press of the olives and, if possible, come back for another squeeze so nothing is wasted, as my old Italian grandmother used to say (only joking, but you get the idea). And if that's not achievable due to time pressures, I like to make sure I've inspected as much as I possibly can before time's up and I have to head home.

THE LOGICAL AND METHODICAL ROUTINE

Logic would suggest that you start at one end of the field and work your way up and down the rows until you've weaved your way through the entire thing, finishing at the very last stall at the opposite end of the field.

Doing that will definitely ensure you cover every inch of ground.

Not only that, but a lot of car boot diehards like to get there at the very outset of proceedings, at 6 or 7 a.m., and then follow the new arrivals as they set up, in the same way that seagulls trail a trawler or pigeons mill around behind a tractor as it ploughs.

And that is certainly another sound plan. You get to see all the new stuff as it arrives, and you're first on the scene as great items are unpacked. You'll be focused only on the new arrivals, though, and you'll be among a jostling morass of hawk-like dealer-types, with curt manners and a belligerent demeanour, who are going all out to get their hands on things before anyone else, and pressuring the hapless sellers in the process. Elbows and barrier-like body language will be everywhere, and the sweat will be on.

From this description you can picture, I hope, the stress of doing this.

In reality, such a modus operandi can be a tiring and frustrating method of attempting to get the most from your visit. And, perhaps counter-intuitively, it doesn't necessarily get you the best bargains anyway.

If you constantly follow the arrivals as they unpack from the very start, you'll be moving on at a faster pace than anyone can possibly hope to lay out their wares, and while you pour all your effort into being first, you'll be missing the chance to see the whole of someone's offering once it's all removed from boxes and bags.

My preferred strategy is to arrive somewhat later than the advertised start time, say 7 a.m. instead of 6 a.m., and then start at the beginning. The 'marauders' are rows and rows ahead of me, but I feel I get to see more of what's available overall, and with considerably fewer people shoving and elbowing me out of the way.

Another idea is, once again, to arrive a little later and work your way backwards from the latest arrival to the first, plodding the rows in the opposite direction to many of your fellow buyers and avoiding the stampede.

This really does work, and I find I always come away with a bagful of great purchases. Okay, so I might have missed a few real peaches at the 'sharp end', but what I haven't seen I'm not exactly going to miss, am I? Plus, I can then return to my starting point and mop up the final few arrivals at the end.

Having said all of this, there is little or no point in arriving at a car boot sale after, say, 9.30–10 a.m. if you expect to pick up really good stuff. Lots of people do arrive at that time, and often much later, but they are only going to get a chance at the leftovers. The ardent, determined buyers will have already cleaned up by that time because, with car boots, the early birds really do get the juiciest worms.

Whichever route you choose, try to stick to your original plan, or else there is a fair chance that you'll miss out on what could be potentially interesting pitches.

When you've been going to car boots for a while, and especially if you attend the same ones week after week, you'll soon learn how to read the 'geography' of the event. By that I mean the placing of certain sellers and the likely position of others.

Obviously, the real regulars, and especially the traders, for whom car boots are a part of their routine weekly selling schedules, will have their preferred spots, and they are most likely to be in the first few rows to set up because they're disciplined people who want to squeeze the maximum benefit out of their time investment. If they don't sell the things you're interested in, it makes it easy to bypass them.

The boot sale 'middle ground' or mid-field will be the temporary home to the keen sellers, who've made the effort to be up bright and early, are properly motivated and really mean business. This is the selling constituent that embraces the potential of the boot sale and wants to trade with you.

As you get further and further towards the other end of the selling space, you will find the Johnny-come-latelys of the event. Many of them aren't parking and unloading their stuff until after 9 a.m., meaning that typically the two hours of prime selling time have already passed. I've been to boots where sellers are arriving as late as 11 a.m. or even midday, at a point when others pitches have been picked bare and most of the possible punters have drifted off home. It's pathetic to see them laying out their wares for an audience that has dwindled to almost nothing.

From a buying viewpoint, though, these dilettante sellers can be a great source of bargains. If they're so disorganised or indolent that they turn up just before closing time, they're unlikely to be on the ball with their prices, meaning that goodies aplenty might be on offer for silly money. The question is, are you yourself going to have the stamina to stick around long enough to find out? If you've been on patrol since before 7 a.m., then by 11 a.m. you could be forgiven for flagging somewhat.

WORKING IT THE OTHER WAY

If the event is a manageable size, or if you have the time available, it's always, always worth retracing the steps of your browsing route in exactly the opposite direction. Like a road or train trip, it's amazing how the terrain of a car boot sale can look totally different on the return journey.

When you come at a stall from the opposite direction, you'll frequently notice items that were seemingly invisible to you the first time round. And, once attracted to something, you may well also notice other goodies you missed before. That could be down to any number of factors, including the angle of sunlight, blocking by other browsers, or even the way the stall has been rearranged in the interim. I've shocked myself by alighting on things that I really should have noticed the first time round but – curiously – didn't.

LIKE IT? THERE MAY BE LOTS MORE WAITING FOR YOU!

Go to a few dozen car boot sales and you'll start to notice something strange happening. You get an intangible sensation, a feeling that is almost like a tingling, when you come across a stall with your kind of items on it. You begin to be able to spot it from 50 metres away.

What could it be down to?

- the colours
- the textures
- the outline
- the arrangement
- the age of the wares
- the demeanour of the vendor
- the sort of car

I have to admit, I am not entirely sure myself. All I know is that I get a 'good feeling' about certain pitches, and that it seems to work in tandem with my instincts. It could be due to one, some or all of the above factors.

When you start to develop this car boot sale 'sixth sense', you will recognise the sensation yourself. And when you know it's coming on, the thing to do is to trust it.

If a stall has one thing you fancy at a price you like, then it will often have more – maybe much more.

Just make sure, when you come across a pitch that presses this mysterious internal button for you, that you take the time to really look through the stuff carefully; leave no box or bag untouched and have a look under the table, at the side of the pitch and also at anything that the vendor might have 'behind the counter'.

It's important to do this straight away, because if you leave it the things might not be there when you return. At a big car boot I might come across, say, five or six such stalls, and they will be the ones at which I 'feast', buying virtually everything on the day from them.

The converse of this is that you will soon be able to recognise those pitches that have absolutely nothing that interests you, and be able to devote less of your precious browsing time to them. For example, if you're looking for clothes for an amateur theatre production, and the guy has mostly tools, spirit levels, chisels and screws to sell – and you've seen him a few times before, usually in the same spot – then this becomes one seller to trot straight past.

SIZING UP THE SELLER
How much can you tell about the vendor and what they

might have to offer on the basis of the quickest sideways glance?

Kerry Ball, car boot clothes expert, is adamant that you can tell what's on offer from a guesstimate of the person's size.

'If I look at a lady who is a size 14, I'm not going to be looking at her clothes because I'm not that size,' she says. 'That might be a mistake but I do tend to judge them by what they're wearing.

'I also look at the car too. If it's an expensive one then that says "money", which means there could be good stuff there – expensive brands. I recently saw a woman with an absolutely gorgeous car, and it really drew me in. I ended up buying half of her stock on the day and then, later, half of her home stock too.'

On the other hand, if you're after retro items for your house, then any elderly people manning a pitch will be a natural reel-in for you. Their idea of what is attractive, interesting and unusual is likely to be skewed by the passage of time and the relative apathy they hold for items they've owned for a long, long time. Folk like this are the natural source of the retro or vintage household items that fill trendy shops in the more bohemian parts of London and other big cities; they simply can't see the appeal of their junk to a new generation, and their stalls give off an aroma of opportunity that, if you have a real feel for this stuff, can be detected a mile off.

WHAT ARE YOU REALLY AFTER, AND IS A CAR BOOT SALE ACTUALLY WORTH YOUR WHILE?

This might seem like quite a fundamental issue to introduce at this stage of the book. But, when all's said and done, everyone wants to spend their time either productively or enjoyably, preferably both.

The joyfully random nature of any car boot event means you simply cannot be certain of what you will or won't find. But if you really do have a very specialist interest, you may have to face disappointment week after week.

This is perhaps less likely for contemporary personal items like clothes, shoes, house wares, entertainment and modern toys, but applies much more to antiques and collectables.

We live in a time when the houses and lofts being cleared of junk by private individuals are unlikely to have lain untouched for much more than fifty years, which takes us back to the mid or early sixties. That means supplies of items from the Art Deco/1930s, Edwardian, Victorian and earlier eras are much reduced compared to what was available in, for instance, 1990. This will apply to every conceivable antique or collectable item; the fact is that the pickings from periods before the fifties are probably going to be small.

Plus, of course, with the large number of daytime TV shows devoted to the concept of cash in the attic, flogging it, and buying antiques on a road trip, many sellers might be tempted to withhold things they perceive as valuable, preferring instead to sell them direct to antique dealers, online or by entering them into an antiques auction.

If it's eighteenth-century porcelain or First World War medals you collect, you may find car boot sales just turn up too little of what you seek. Your time might be better spent at London auction houses or specialist collectors' fairs, or maybe by trawling the Internet with its easy ability to narrow things down. So, overall, when it comes to buying rare, ancient or particularly special things at car boots, you should be prepared for surprises but, equally, you shouldn't expect them.

CHAPTER 17
Bargaining

One of the most frequent issues I hear aired from people who have sold at car boot sales is that they find it hard to cope with brazen bargainers. To that I say: deal with it!

Anyone who buys at car boot sales is absolutely entitled to offer whatever they like – and don't you forget it!

The sanitised lives we all live these days include fewer and fewer opportunities for us to experience proper market mechanisms first-hand. Maybe that's because so many of us are divorced from the means of production. You know, children thinking milk comes from supermarkets and not cows, and adults not understanding that pylons bring nuclear-generated power to our homes so we can watch telly.

The fact is, many of us are so used to queuing up at Homebase or Asda and paying for whatever the scanned barcode demands that we are made inhibited and nervous by the concept of engaging a seller in a bargaining situation. This is an inhibition you need to lose, and fast.

Almost everything you'll come across at a car boot is second-hand. And second-hand goods have no set values. They are worth only what someone is prepared to accept for them, moderated by what another person is willing to offer.

Sellers in general seem to have little or no idea how to price what they have for sale. The only guide they have is what they themselves paid for something when it was new, and they are hardly in an objective position to decide what its value is after their period of ownership and usage.

This is, of course, the reason why a sizeable majority of car boot sellers won't put price tickets on their goods. Of course, many simply don't have the time to do it and others can't be bothered, but yet more wouldn't know what to charge. And that, of course, just adds to the overall impression that everything is open to an offer. It's all to play for.

So…you probably see where this is heading, don't you…

Don't be afraid of making an offer

And, furthermore:

Don't be afraid of making a silly offer

And, even more so:

Don't be afraid of making a downright cheeky offer

Remember:

- Very little is pre-priced at a car boot.

- Most private sellers are here to get rid.

- Offers are the name of the game.

- Second-hand goods have no set value – they're worth what someone is prepared to accept.

- If you don't go for it then someone else will.

If you're feeling even slightly apprehensive about making offers, then look around you and see what other people are doing. Yes, that's right, they're busy making offers.

The overriding protocol goes like this: the buyer alights on what they fancy; they hold it up to get the seller's attention; they ask, 'How much is this?'; the price is delivered…sometimes after quite a few seconds of 'think' time; the potential new owner either a) puts it down and carries on browsing, b) walks off, in which case one must assume that the asking price was so high as to be unchallengeable, or c) the potential new owner makes an offer somewhere in the range between reasonable and rude. At that stage, the offer is – more often than not – accepted. Or it is declined, and then further offers are made until either a deal is struck, or the seller digs in his or her heels and the item remains unsold.

The important thing to remember is that the majority of scenarios are likely to end in your offer being accepted and you getting the thing for the price you're prepared to pay.

So don't be at all held back by the verbal tussle of the process.

HOW LOW SHOULD I GO?

Well, before we even begin to tackle the percentage business, here I should make at least one plea on behalf of the pleasant, honest amateur seller.

If you ask a price and you pretty much like what you hear – if it's already an absolute steal, is in tip-top condition and it's just what you've been looking for – then do the decent thing and pay it. Everyone will have a warm feeling and you'll be oiling the wheels of the system from which you've just greatly benefited. If it's something unusual that you know all about but of which the seller seems completely ignorant, then all your specialist knowledge has come into play and you've lucked out. Pay the lady or gentleman, and be glad.

Good, so that's enough Mr Nice Guy. If you think you can get it for less, then let the haggling begin.

When it comes to house buying, we generally knock off the anticipated cost of repairs before making an offer, but healthy demand in many areas of the UK means that the old days of making offers well below the asking price for no other reason than 'sport' don't get you very far any more. In another area, when you buy a car you should routinely expect to be able to chip between 5 and 15 per cent off the asking price, as that is already factored into the dealer's margins even before any serious maladies are identified.

But in a field full of miscellaneous second-hand goods, you could go much further.

In many cases, you could simply cut the asking price in half, and see where that gets you – the price is given as £1 but you offer 50p, or £4 and you suggest £2.

Too impertinent?

Well, I've done that on many occasions and on a good third of them have been successful straight away. The seller runs it through his or her mental computer, decides that clearing the decks trumps holding out for more, and says yes.

But if you think that's jammy, you haven't seen some of the buyers in operation.

Many of the car boots I go to attract a huge number of people for whom English is not their first language. It's hard to generalise, of course, and no English-versus-foreigners axe is being ground, but it does appear that some of them are used to very hard bargaining, perhaps in real life situations where, in the immortal phrase from Monty Python's *Life of Brian*, 'you've got to haggle'.

Some of these people react to an initial price with an offer of a quarter of the sum and work their way up to paying half. What's more, it's rarely done with charm. Some of these people can be positively curt. It's not pretty, and many sellers get visibly riled, but it's amazing how often the buyer gets the item at an absolute snip, possibly because the seller crumples and capitulates at such effrontery.

From your viewpoint as a buyer, these people are to be admired rather than detested. They prove what can be done if you go in hard. But you may need to make yourself bolder than you actually feel, so take a leaf from their books. It may not feel comfortable, but why not? After all...

You probably won't see this person ever again...

...And that means that if they react badly to you, then so what?

And, of course, they don't have to sell it to you, do they?

They can just say 'No', scowl at you, and the moment passes.

Still, we're British, and most of us are pretty polite. I'd bet that most people reading this will feel comfortable in making an offer that's about two thirds of the asking price, with an expectation that we'll take it for about a quarter less. The suggestion of a 33 per cent discount would be highly unlikely to upset anyone, and that is a level at which your offer is highly likely to simply be accepted as it stands, rather than being tickled upwards by the seller.

You may know full well that a collectable item you enquire about is worth only £1 when the vendor is asking £10. That 90 per cent is quite a chasm to overcome. The seller is ignorant of the market rate for the thing, and has made up the price on the basis of you know not what, or guesswork. You might simply have to walk away, but it's always worth making a mental note of the thing, and returning at packing-up time. If the object is still there, he might just let it go for something more reasonable, which in his mind might be £2. If it's a nice example, you may as well have it, even if for a little more than you hoped to pay, because you could kick yourself afterwards for holding back for the sake of a third of the price of a cappuccino from a high-street coffee shop.

That's the thing about car booting. It is easy to lose all sense of perspective. When we go supermarket shopping we pile our trolleys full of stuff and barely notice the individual price of things. So the impact of an expensive cake is blunted by the cheap cost of some onions. But try buying individual things from high street outlets and suddenly you feel the separate 'pinch'. The hot beverage just mentioned is one that always gets me: £3 for something that wouldn't cost 3p to make at home. It's even more noticeable for a ready-made sandwich at three quid when you could buy all the ingredients for ten of them for the same price. And when buying a round of drinks in the pub, you can immediately kiss goodbye to a £10 or £20 note.

These things put the meagre sums asked for items at a car boot – £5 for a pair of jeans, £2 for a DVD, a quid for a mug – into perspective, and should act as your bellwether against being too stingy. Refuse to shell out that extra pound at the time but 'waste' a pound on a chocolate bar later, and it soon becomes obvious that truly mean-spirited bargaining doesn't always make rational sense.

IS IT DAMAGED? IS SOMETHING MISSING?

Quite a few of the things you chance upon at a car boot

sale will not be as good as new. That almost goes without saying. But if that piece of china has a chip, a jumper is snagged or a toy has a part missing, these are all grounds for a good discount.

Make sure you examine your potential purchases carefully, and point out any issues, breakages or absent parts.

The vendor may or may not be aware that there is a fault with the item. But you, on the other hand, might not see this as a problem, because you know you can mend, fix, straighten, renovate or complete at home. Don't point out that the problem isn't of great concern. Instead, adopt an expression somewhere between concern and grave doubt. If the seller sees that you're still prepared to buy it, at a vastly reduced price, they will still want to sell it to you; if they feel it can't be flogged off to you personally, then they'll most likely have to go through the same unproductive process with the next punter that chances on it. All of which increases the urgency to get something, anything, for it, and preferably from you, the person currently weighing up its questionable merits.

THE 'JOB LOT'

This is indeed a phrase that can exert a powerful magic. Offering to relieve a seller of a good quantity of what they have for sale can bring enormous dividends. No matter what they had in mind in terms of individual prices, once you start gathering a heap of items, those best-laid plans can be torn up.

There are two approaches.

The first one is where you point to a bag or box of items and simply ask: 'How much for the whole lot?'

In most instances, this is likely to catch the seller off-balance, as it isn't a buyer's usual pattern. But if they're smart, they won't want to miss this opportunity and let you wander off empty-handed. In this instance, they are making the offer to you and the bargaining only begins with any counter-offer you feel you can get away with. If the person is serious about clearing the decks, you'll be in a strong position to get what you want.

And if this is one or two peachy items among a group of other things that you could definitely do something with, then it will be worthwhile. In fact, even if you were to sling the secondary things away, or recycle them when you get home, you still might get the items you want for less than if you'd tried to knock the price down on them alone.

The second approach is where you select several things, or even a great many, from the seller's selection, and gradually build up a heap of stuff you want before the widening eyes of the vendor. Obviously, this will depend very much on the display consisting largely of things that you want, which could be because the seller shares very much your taste, or else there just happens to be a range of diverse objects which take your fancy.

Pick your moment
However you identify what it is you want to buy, choosing your moment to make an offer for a job lot will be important. You stand least chance at the start of play, really any

time before 9 a.m., because sellers will realise there is still plenty of selling time left and no shortage of new potential buyers to descend on their goods. But come 10–10.30 a.m., when many sellers have been on their feet for more than three hours and the intensity of buyer interest has cooled down from the initial frenzy, the worry that they're not going to shift everything starts to build, so from that moment on becomes the time to strike.

You'll notice exactly which sellers are semi-regulars, and therefore not concerned with selling everything on the spot because they'll be returning, by the reaction to your job lot offer price. Some will certainly not want to play ball. But as the clock ticks towards 11 a.m., and then on to midday, many sellers will be falling over themselves to do deals on sales of a whole lot of their wares.

When it comes to making your actual offer, as before, don't be afraid to set an insultingly low asking price. For all the reasons previously mentioned, you're in a strong position. In fact, if it's late in the morning and the event is heading for shutdown, then you're calling the shots. Whatever it is that you think the job lot is worth, knock another third off, so that you have the margin to build back up to, and you can close at the price you had in mind.

AND WHAT ABOUT...EVERYTHING?

I've never actually witnessed this, but I assume it must have happened a few times. You make an offer for absolutely everything the person has for sale. It could, for sure, bring you a mega bargain, assuming you were prepared to later dispose of the undoubted bits of detritus that would be part of any such deal. Remember, this would present a uniquely attractive prospect to any seller, who can now sling their table into the back of their car, count their cash and call it a day. But then, of course, their problem has become your problem, so you'd better have a well worked-out plan of what you intend to do with it all. It would be, naturally, the job lot of all job lots.

OVERALL

If I haven't got over the message that you should bargain hard, make low offers and generally take advantage of the pressing need for most sellers to sell their things in the very limited time available, then I have failed. Remember: you can still be courteous while discarding all your inhibitions about insulting anyone. Act bolder than, perhaps, you may feel inside. Offers are the name of the game, and if you don't get what you want for a bargain price that suits, there will most likely be someone right behind you who will grab the opportunity you've just wasted.

CHAPTER 18

Quick decisions and 'special requests'

It doesn't matter how many decades you've been going to car boot sales, every 'old hand' experiences that sinking feeling when they wish they'd bought something they passed over.

At any event your eye will pass over literally thousands of different items, scanning more slowly over anything that pushes the right buttons, and halting occasionally on objects that really do hit the spot.

After a few months of practice, you'll barely notice that you've developed a sophisticated inner quality-control system and that you don't even pick anything up that isn't a possible purchase.

When you reach this tricky-to-define plateau of discernment, though, it does tend to mean that almost everything you're drawn towards is something you want.

And if you don't go for it then and there, you could kick yourself for not bagging it.

DON'T HESITATE

How soon after you've looked at something with border-line appeal do you go back to grab it? My advice is not to leave it beyond departing that very aisle of stalls. Your antennae are probably already twitching backwards. But once you've left the 'ley line' along which this gem is positioned, you could have real trouble relocating it.

I used to have this notion of completing the first mine sweep of an event before then backtracking to reconsider items for which a purchase decision had been a near thing. But often, and despite methodically retracing my steps, it has proved absolutely impossible to find that item again. Not just the thing itself, but sometimes even the stall it was on.

It happened to me just the other day. I spotted a superb vintage 1960s Thermos flask with a great retro pattern on the outside and all its components in great original condition, but just couldn't decide whether the £8 asking price was a negotiable starting point or not. I didn't have the guts to start with the £4 offer that would lead to the fiver I'd be willing to exchange for it.

Having then reached the end of the final row, I changed my mind and decided to return to bag the Thermos. It was impossible. Despite my memory of it being bright red, tall and upright, on a table of white and beige bric-a-brac, I just couldn't find it. I tried to recall the faces of the husband-and-wife sellers, what sort of car they had, how far down the row their pitch was, whether it was near the base of a telegraph pole or adjacent to a large blue van, what the stuff looked like on the groundsheet in front of the table.

But all to no avail. I simply couldn't find it. Okay, it might have sold in the interim, but that was no less a frustration.

You will think you can insert a mental bookmark into the layout of the car boot sale, but in reality it can be very hard indeed to remember exactly where something was. So...

If you see something that you want, or even think you want, take a few seconds to stand still and decide there and then that you either will go for it or that you are happy to pass over the opportunity and, as far as you're concerned, you won't be heartbroken if you can't return to it.

If you do want it, then follow all the advice given previously about bargaining hard for a good final price. But do it with confidence; as you've trusted your instincts, now make sure you come to a swift agreement on the money. You may have weighed up the pros and cons, and made the decision that on balance you should buy it, but as far as the seller is concerned, you're just another customer.

Work on the basis that if you don't grab something when you first see it, you'll never see it again, either literally or metaphorically. True, it takes several tortuous experiences like what I now call 'The Lost Thermos Incident' for this to sink in, but you soon learn that it's the only surefire way not to miss out on all the things you might fancy.

KEEP YOUR COOL IF YOU CHANCE UPON 'THE BIG ONE'
Tales of hyper-valuable artworks and antiques found for a few pounds at car boot sales are legion. Here are five absolute corkers:

- In 2009, a seventeenth-century still life by Dutch painter Edwaert Collier was bought for £1 at a car boot in Sudbury, Suffolk, and sold for £29,000 at auction.

- In 2011, three eighteenth-century drinking glasses made by the renowned glassmaker William Beilby were bought for 40p from a car boot sale in Portsmouth, and sold for £18,880 at auction.

- In 2011, a handwritten letter from Paul McCartney inviting a drummer to join his new band the Beatles in 1960 was bought for 50p from a car boot sale in Bootle, Liverpool (it was found tucked inside a book), and sold for £35,000 at auction.

- In 2013, a 1922 Royal Doulton 'Spook' figurine was bought for £2 at a car boot sale in Stockport, Cheshire, and sold for £4,250 at an auction filmed by BBC One's *Flog It* show.

- In 2013, a Breitling Top Time watch uniquely modified for use by Sean Connery in the James Bond movie *Thunderball* was bought for £25 at an undisclosed car boot sale and sold for £103,875 at auction.

I can only dream of purchases like these, although I've had my fair share of good finds. I picked up a rare Swiss-made 1950s Marvin advertising watch for £1 that I sold for £60, a Land Rover workshop manual for £1 that I sold for £78, and a £3 bag of early 1980s action models of characters in the 1980s *M.A.S.K.* TV cartoon series, which, when cleaned up and sold off individually, made more than £100. More typical might be rare books or old toys for which I pay between 50p and £1 a time and sell for £10–15.

This book was never intended to be a guide on how to make millions from buying. Those kinds of books tend to be unrealistic dream-stokers; you can't help wondering that if it was really achievable, why isn't the author doing it rather than writing about it? Anyway, I'm not sure such 'advice' can ever be imparted in a single volume because, as you may have gleaned from the examples highlighted above, most cheap items that turn out to be highly valuable are not fluke finds but are identified as the result of the incredibly detailed specialist knowledge the buyer has accumulated.

If you're ever fortunate enough to chance across something on offer for a few pence that you know is worth five figures, just be careful not to let your excitement boil over. And certainly never get out your mobile to start checking online in front of the vendor; you might give the game away. Look impassive, even slightly bored or resigned…but keep the item close to you, or better still, in hand so no one else can snatch it from you. Make doubly sure you don't leave the scene of your epic discovery without taking time to thoroughly double-check there isn't something else from the same seller lurking nearby that's in the same vein. Pay up and stroll off, trying extremely hard not to leap in the air shouting, 'Yes! Yes!'

TO LUG OR NOT TO LUG?

Most car boot buyers associate these vibrant market places with small, portable items that can be transported in a pocket, a carrier bag or a holdall.

But whether you anticipate it or not, a lot of 'big stuff' does turn up for sale, brought along in vans, small lorries or on trailers.

I've seen plenty of the bigger pieces of household furniture, including sofas, beds and dining tables, but I've also seen such heavyweight items as toilets, baths and washbasins, as well as fridges, dishwashers and cookers and, in one instance, a small kiln. Bicycles, prams/pushchairs, planters/urns, doors, window frames and lawnmowers are the bulky items you'll encounter most frequently – all of which are readily identifiable as 'consumer' products – but there could be any number or variety of other large things that could be brought along on the off-chance the right buyer could turn up.

You yourself might attend with some of these things on your mind, and chances are that you'll pick up something worthwhile. I bought my lawnmower, an old petrol-powered Qualcast, in just such circumstances. I'd been vaguely looking for something similar to put stripes into my lawn and which I could be justly proud of in that pathetic male way, and suddenly there it was. The seller fired it up, the blades sliced their way effectively through the grass it was sitting on, and I handed over forty quid. Fortunately, I'd arrived that day in a van-shaped estate car, and I managed to get it home without bringing on a hernia.

However, I wasn't going to wheel the beast around the rest of the event with me. So I paid the seller and he agreed to hold on to it for me until it was time to go.

Did I feel nervous about handing over four tenners to a complete stranger when not taking my purchase with me? The answer is no, not at all. I have never come across a situation where a seller won't do this. This particular guy's van was well sandwiched in by other cars, so there was no chance he could do a runner while I was away. And, in fact, a couple of people have independently told me that a large 'eye point' item that dominates a pitch is useful to them, whether it's sold or not – as I mention on page 81. A prominent object cannot fail but to draw the attention of the passing browser, and once it's on the stall he or she will linger for longer while examining what else is on offer.

The thing is, an item doesn't have to be that big to be too unwieldy to carry as you search the rest of the boot fair. Even a couple of cushions or a dog bed could be cumbersome purchases to cart about, and other things could be portable but weighty.

Once you've paid, don't be nervous to ask if it can be put aside for you. Most people will be willing to tuck it somewhere inside their car. But remember:

- If you don't feel 100 per cent sure about the seller, ask for a receipt for your cash.

- Make a note of the pitch number, or the number of the aisle and the approximate position of the vendor manning it, so you can easily make your way back there later.

- In addition, take a note of the person's vehicle registration number, or take a snap of it with your phone.

- Fix a rough time when you intend to return to claim your newly acquired property, and make sure you stick to it.

MEETING UP 'OUT OF SCHOOL'

I am certainly no advocate of meeting up with a seller away from the car boot sale arena. If that's something you feel happy doing, that's entirely up to you.

But as I said in Chapter 8, sellers do sometimes have an annoying tendency of telling you that they have things at home you might be interested in and if only they had brought them. A fat lot of good that is at the time, but it's possible that you may want to get in touch with the person at a later date and, maybe, meet up to conclude some sort of private arrangement.

If the seller is happy to give you their number so that you can contact them later, then fine. If you choose to give them your details, that is also good, just as long as you feel secure enough to do so. The safest method would probably be to give a mobile number and your first name.

Even that is no guarantee that the exchange will lead anywhere. I once gave my details to some chap who told me that he had hundreds more vintage car magazines taking up space at home in addition to the handful he had on his stall (which I bought anyway), and that he was extremely keen to find someone to take them off his hands for a reasonable sum.

I never heard from the bloke again. Such is life.

CHAPTER 19
Things to avoid

In Chapter 5 you can find out all about the small number of things that stallholders are not allowed to sell. As a buyer, though, you are considerably freer of legal obligations.

The areas where there are age-related restrictions, such as alcohol, tobacco and imitation firearms, are all pertinent, as no one under the age of 18 is allowed to purchase these things. However, no one at a car boot sale should ever be selling them either. And even if they had a licence to do so legally by some means, they should never be offered to under-eighteens.

For buyers, it is more a question of what items to avoid out of choice, and with a large dollop of that old-fashioned and legally nebulous attribute: common sense. Here are a few of the areas where you'd be well advised to take great care, or else to accept the risk that is inherent in the purchase of them.

ELECTRICAL GOODS
Consumer advice offered by the Government highlights three specific items, all electrical, that should be very much

avoided in a second-hand state and/or bought from someone unfamiliar to you:

- Electric fires
- Electric blankets
- Irons

It should be obvious to any adult that these products contain live electricity and heating elements and are likely to be used in close proximity to people. The risks in using these appliances when you don't know where they have come from – they don't have a 'reputable, recent source', in the words of the official Trading Standards guidance – are dangerously high. Strictly speaking, it is not illegal to buy them – just extremely stupid.

And beyond these key danger areas, you should be extremely cautious of anything involving a mains plug and/or electrical wiring. That means everything from the simplest lamp and small kitchen gadgets, like toasters, kettles, juicers and mixers, up to larger and more unusual contraptions, such as foot spas, TVs and even computers and toys.

If you have electrical qualifications, or you've done a relevant Portable Appliance Testing (PAT) course and have the appropriate testing equipment, then you may feel much more confident that you can verify the item is in good and safe working order. If you are not certain, or confident, then by all means buy the item but make absolutely sure you have it looked at by someone who knows what they're doing before you start using it. If you have any doubts at all at the browsing stage, simply give the thing a wide berth.

FOODSTUFFS

The hidden dangers in food and drink whose provenance you are unsure of should be clear to every adult with a logical mind. You might take the greatest of care over the hygiene in the family kitchen when it comes to the storage, preparation and cooking of food, being vigilant in your effort to prevent food poisoning and the spread of dangerous bacteria. But if you're considering buying edible products from a stranger, how can you know whether or not they've adhered to the same standards?

The answer, of course, is that you can't. And while you may feel completely at ease buying homemade jam, chutney or cakes from Women's Institute members at your local village fete, can you feel similarly confident with a henna-haired woman in a hoody with a fag in one hand and the other being licked by her pit bull terrier?

Avoid all prepared or processed food on sale by private sellers – as opposed to caravans and mobile snack bars on-site, which will (or should have) been given a hygiene certificate by the local authority.

I've often seen rows of cupcakes, éclairs, strawberry tarts and other tempting confectionery treats lined up on stalls, and I've inwardly winced at the number of people who lean over them to take a look. I'm not saying that they've actually drooled, sneezed, coughed or exhaled over them, but I can't be entirely sure about that either. Not for nothing are similarly 'freshly made' items displayed behind glass in the supermarket. So think on.

You can make an exception for fresh fruit and veg that might be on sale from the 'pop-up' greengrocers who seem to be at most car boot sales these days. It may not be true in all cases, but I'm guessing that many of these sellers have a market stall during the week, and that a car boot is the last chance to dispose of stock that is reaching the end of its shelf life, and must henceforth be disposed of. Most experienced food shoppers and foodies will be able to get an instant idea of the quality of this produce simply by looking at it, so deception isn't really an issue. Just make sure that whatever you buy in this line is subjected to a very good wash before it's cooked or consumed, as you'll have no idea where it has spent the previous week.

Quick five-a-day ad!
NB: I should just say here that vegetables and fruit sold at car boots can offer excellent value for money, and that the sellers are inclined to be generous if you're buying in bulk. One chirpy Cockney regular I'm familiar with sells a veritable armful of bananas for virtually nothing, and when I've asked for just one to keep me going as I browse, he gives it to me for nothing. If you find a gem of a produce seller like this, why not make him or her your shopping destination for the weekly fresh fruit 'n' veg shop, and save a small fortune on your household outgoings? Ahem, anyway, back to the 'avoids'.

KIDS' STUFF

When you buy clothes, shoes and toys for your offspring from high street shops, you can be pretty certain that what they sell is of a merchantable quality and, most of all, safe. No high-street brand wants a scandal that shows they neglect product safety, and the speed with which goods are recalled if a problem is identified is a clear indication of how seriously they take the safeguarding of their reputation.

Plenty of these goods, which might have been unattainable and high-priced for many when they were new, eventually find their way to car boot sales when they are no longer needed, ready to provide service and pleasure to someone else.

However, a good deal of caution should be exercised when buying for the use of children.

This is because the route that various items take before they arrive at the car boot means there may well be things on sale that do not meet modern safety standards. Or perhaps they are items that weren't originally sold new in the UK and therefore haven't been subjected to strict retail regulations.

- Night clothes: these might be made from materials that are too easily flammable.

- Cords: clothes with cords or drawstrings might present the possible risk of strangulation.

- Zips, buttons, clasps: all these things, if poorly designed, manufactured or fitted, could present hazards.

- Toys and games: if these are second-rate, cheap imitations or counterfeits, they could break easily, exposing sharp edges or points.

This last category – toys and games – is one to be especially aware of. And never more so than if you are touring the car boot with small children in tow.

Reputable manufacturers go to seemingly enormous lengths to make sure that their products are suitable for children in carefully defined age ranges. The difficulty for buyers of second-hand examples is that such information is usually communicated on the packaging rather than the toy itself, and that packaging is more than likely to be missing.

That puts the onus on you, doubtless the parent or other relative, to make sure that any toys you pick up are not only suitable for their intended end users in terms of minimum age, but are also in a good enough condition not to cause any undue harm.

CONCLUSION

Buying carefully is all about avoiding certain specific items with unknown or unknowable provenance. Instances of harm caused by ill-informed purchases are, thankfully, very rare, because the vast majority of buyers use their common sense when deciding what to buy. Make sure that applies to you.

THE FINAL CUT?

Back in Chapter 15 we looked at your essential 'kit' for car booting, and mentioned protective gloves as a possible asset.

Almost every car boot sale will have a good number of sellers who've brought along boxes, tins or bags of old tools, fixings, metal attachments and small machines. Quite a few others might have large quantities of cutlery and kitchen equipment in containers, with all sorts of things that might interest you buried deep among them.

If you know you'll be drawn to stuff like this then taking a pair of tough work gloves with you – the kind that you might wear when trimming a thorny hedge or handling wood covered in nails or splinters – is a really sound plan.

I have sustained several cuts to fingertips and scraped my knuckles badly when rummaging through really disorganised pitches, and I've drawn blood from the jagged metal edges of rusty tins and from kitchen knives. Fortunately, no long-term damage was done, but this kind of contact is never intentional, and you don't want to slice yourself on something that's really sharp. So wear your gloves when delving into the depths of anything metallic.

And be very aware of the broken glass, china or plastic that might lurk in boxes or packing cases. Many sellers simply don't bother to separate out even quite brittle or delicate things like these – you get this a lot in unsorted, hurriedly filled boxes of house clearance items especially – and they often get broken by accident as people carelessly churn their way through difficult-to-access containers.

IS IT STOLEN?
It is illegal to handle stolen goods but, as the buyer, you are

hardly likely to be culpable in this; it will be the seller who is guilty, even if unwittingly.

Trading Standards suggests that you should 'beware of popular items of stolen property'. By which, of course, they mean don't buy it, and they're referring to items such as:

- Bicycles

- Power tools

- Lawnmowers

- Garden equipment

- Garden décor and fixtures

They're talking, of course, about good-quality, high-value stuff that's been nicked from gardens, sheds, summer houses, garages and lock-ups – the sort of more-than-petty thefts which are reported in those depressing little stories that pepper every local paper in the land.

Quite how you are expected to know that the goods in question have been stolen is a tough call. Most of us, perhaps, could hazard a guess by taking stock of the relationship between the appearance of the vendor, the quality of the 'gear', the other stuff on sale and the status of the vehicle it's been transported in. Not every unshaven and shifty-looking person is a guaranteed villain, of course, but if you have your suspicions, then avoid. If the item does turn out to have been stolen and it's recovered from you then you won't be getting a refund. And obviously, of course, if you do have a genuine reason to suspect that stolen goods are being sold, it's your duty to alert the police in an inconspicuous way. You'll be doing your bit to rid car boots of the criminal element which can sully the reputation of your favourite sales arena.

Appendix

The UK's biggest: A selection of the biggest and most popular boot sales, and useful website addresses

As there are, by some measures, up to 2,000 car boot-type events staged around the UK in any given week, you should never have any trouble finding one close to where you are.

I'm not even going to try to attempt to give details of all of them. For one thing, events – even old established ones – come and go. Some organisers retire or decide to hang up their hats, while other hopefuls constantly emerge. To get the most up-to-date information you should always look first in digital media, and if not then your local newspaper.

However, I have decided to list for you one-hundred car boot sales that are well worth considering for both selling and buying activity. As you can see, they are from all over the land, from pretty much every county and with more events listed for areas with high population density.

I've paid special attention to including the biggest events that will both attract the most possible buyers and, if you're a buying visitor, will give you the greatest amount of stuff to browse through. I haven't been to them all, but I sure as hell would like to, given enough time. And the start times, by the way, are all for the beginning of seller set-up time – buyers generally are expected to attend about an hour later. Whatever your reason for going, enjoy the experience.

And to make it easier to find the nearest and most convenient car boots to you, at the very end are a whole bunch of addresses for car boot directory websites. Some are better than others, and there are many more listings to be found online, but www.carbootjunction.com in particular is a masterclass in listing thoroughness and ease of use (they didn't pay me to say that, either).

Bedfordshire
Lidlington Car Boot Sale: on the A507 at the top of the hill, Lidlington MK43 0QR and Westmead Farm, on the old A421 between Marston Moretaine and Brogborough MK43 0SF; www.lidlingtoncarboot.co.uk – Sundays, from 10.30 a.m.

Berkshire
Taplow-Maidenhead Giant Car Boot: opposite Taplow station on the main A4 Bath Road, Maidenhead SL6 0NP; www.giantcarboot.co.uk/taplow – Sundays, 10 a.m.–4 p.m.

Bristol
Clifton: The Clanage, Clanage Road, Bower Ashton BS3 2JX; www.cliftoncarbootsale.com – Sundays, from 8.30 a.m.

Buckinghamshire
Denham: Denham Roundabout, A40, UB9 5PG; www.giantcarboot.co.uk/denham – Saturdays and Good Friday, 9 a.m.–3 p.m.

Cambridgeshire

Huntingdon Racecourse: Brampton, Huntingdon PE28 4NL;
www.giantboots.co.uk – Saturdays and Sundays, from 9.30 a.m.

The Big Boot: Wellington Street Car Park, Peterborough PE1 5DU;
www.bizzybootsltd.co.uk – Sundays, from 11 a.m.

Cheshire

Cheshire Car Boot Sale: The Cheshire Lounge (Nags Head),
A556 Chester Road, Little Millington, Altrincham WA14 3RX;
www.cheshirecarbootsale.com
– Sundays and Bank Holidays, from 6 a.m.

Cornwall

Rosudgeon Car Boot Sale: Rosudgeon & Kenneggy Sports Club,
A394 main Helston Road TR20 9QE; www.rosudgeoncarboot.co.uk
– Wednesdays, from 7 a.m.

Looe Lions Car Boot Sale: West Waylands Farm, Polperro Road,
Looe PL13 2JR – Sundays, 8 a.m.–12 noon.

County Durham

Giant Car Boot Sale: Sedgefield Racecourse, Racecourse Road,
Sedgefield TS21 2HW; www.sedgefield-racecourse.co.uk
– Sundays, 9 a.m.–1 p.m.

Darlington: The Northern Echo Arena, Neasham Road, Darlington,
Durham DL2 1DL – Sundays, from 8 a.m.

Cumbria

Country Car Boot Sale: Lough Farm, Brisco, Carlisle, Cumbria
CA4 0RD – Sundays, from 7 a.m.

Derbyshire

Tansley Car Boot Sale & Sunday Market: Tansley Crossroads, A615 Alfreton to Matlock road, Tansley, Matlock, Derbyshire DE55 6DB – Sundays, 7 a.m.–4 p.m.

Chesterfield Car Boot Sale: The Proact Stadium, 1866 Sheffield Road, Whittington Moor, Chesterfield S41 8NZ; www.theproactstadium.co.uk – Sundays, from 8 a.m.

Devon

Exeter Sunday Market & Car Boot Sale: Matford Centre, Matford Park Road, Marsh Barton, Exeter EX2 8FD; www.exeter.gov.uk – Sundays, 8.45 a.m.–12.45 p.m.

Car Boot Sale: on the A361 main Barnstaple-Braunton road, Pottington EX31 1GE; www.thebestof.co.uk/local/barnstaple – Sundays, from 1 p.m.

Dorset

Ashley Heath: Homeland Farm, Three Legged Cross, Wimborne BN21 6QZ; www.carbootsale.uk.com – Sundays, from 6.30 a.m.

Essex

Dunton: Basildon CM12 9TZ, www.duntoncarbootsale.com – Sundays, 5.30am–2pm, and Wednesdays, 6.30 a.m.–1 p.m.

Giant Car Boot Sale: Stevensons Farm, Southend Arterial Road (A127), Nevendon SS14 3JH; www.nevendonbootsale.com – Thursdays, Sundays and Bank Holiday Mondays, from 8 a.m.

North Weald Market & Car Boot: North Weald Airfield, Merlin Way, Epping CM16 6HR; www.hughmark.co.uk – Saturdays and Bank Holiday Mondays, from 9 a.m.

Harlow Car Boot Sale: Barrows Road Car Park, Pinnacles Industrial Estate, Harlow CM19 5FA; www.countrysidepromotions.co.uk – Sundays, 9 a.m.–4 p.m.

Gloucestershire
Wooton Monster: New Road (B4058), Wotton-under-Edge GL12 8JW; www.monstercarbootsale.co.uk – Sundays and Bank Holiday Mondays, from 12 noon.

Racecourse Boot Sale: Cheltenham Racecourse, Evesham Road, Prestbury, Cheltenham GL50 4SH; www.racecoursebootsale.com – Sundays, 9 a.m.–1 p.m.

Hampshire
Farnborough: Pinehurst Car Park, Farnborough GU14 6YA; www.townandcountrymarkets.co.uk – Sundays, 11 a.m–3 p.m.

Bursledon: Tesco roundabout, Southampton SO31 8GN; www.bursledoncarbootsale.co.uk – Sundays, 6 a.m.–3 p.m.

Basingstoke: The Vyne Community School, Vyne Road, Basingstoke RG21 5PB; www.vyne.hants.sch.uk/community/Car Boot – Sundays and Bank Holiday Mondays, 7.30 a.m.–1 p.m.

Herefordshire
Madley Car Boot Sale: Stoney Street, Madley HR2 9NJ; www. madleycarboot.co.uk – Sundays, from 1.30 p.m.

Hertfordshire

Hatfield Car Boot Sale: Birchwood Sports Centre, Longmead,
Hatfield AL10 0AN; www.countrysidepromotions.co.uk
– Sundays and Bank Holiday Mondays, 10 a.m.–2 p.m.

Hemel Hempstead Car Boot Sale: A4147 Link Road, Hemel
Hempstead HP2 6JH; www.seasonaleventsltd.co.uk
– Saturdays, from 9 a.m.

Giant Outdoor Car Boot Sale: Little Bushey Lane (behind Costco),
corner of Hartspring Lane, Bushey, Watford WD25 8JS
– Sundays, 10 a.m.–2 p.m.

Isle Of Wight

Ryde Car Boot Sale: Quay Road Car Park, Seafront Esplanade, next
to Ryde Superbowl, Ryde PO33 2EL – Sundays, from 11.30 a.m.

Kent

Hayes: Hayes Farm, Hayes Lane, Bromley BR2 7LB;
www.hayesstfarm.co.uk – Sundays, from 6 a.m.

Gigantic Super Boot: Pedham Place, on the A20 at the top of
Farningham Hill, Swanley BR8 8PP; www.smbbootsales.co.uk
– Sundays, from 6 a.m.

Addington Boot Fair: Meadow Crest Farm, London Road,
Addington, West Malling ME19 5DD – Saturdays, from 6.30 a.m.

Canterbury Boot Fair: Wincheap Park & Ride, Ten Perch Road,
Canterbury CT1 3TQ; www.canterbury.gov.uk/leisure-countryside
– Sundays, from 5.30 a.m.

Lancashire

Whyndyke: Whyndyke Farm, Preston New Road, Blackpool
FY4 4XQ; www.blackpoolcarboot.co.uk –Sundays, from 7.30 a.m.

Giant Indoor Market & Car Boot Sale: Carrs Industrial Estate,
Bentwood Road, Haslingdon, Rossendale BB4 5EJ;
www.carbootsalerossendale.co.uk – daily, 7 a.m.–2 p.m.

Burscough Giant Car Boot Sale: Burscough Airfield, Tollgate Road,
Burscough, Ormskirk L40 7TG and The Showground, Pippin Street,
Burscough, Ormskirk L40 7SP and White Dial Farm, Moss Lane,
Burscough, Ormskirk L40 4AT; www.carbootnorthwest.com
– Sundays, from 5 a.m.

Leicestershire

Measham: Bosworth Road, Measham DE12 7HA;
www.meashamcarboot.co.uk
– Sundays and Bank Holiday Mondays, 6.30 a.m.–1 p.m.

Saddington: Limes Farm LE8 0RJ, and White Stacks Farm LE8 0HJ,
both between Kibworth and Saddington; www.carboot.info
– Sundays and Bank Holiday Mondays, from 6 a.m.

Lincolnshire

Hemswell: Hemswell Cliff, Caenby Corner, between Lincoln and
Scunthorpe DN21 5TJ; www.hemswellmarket.co.uk
– Sundays, 6.30a.m.–3p.m.

Bottesford Giant Car Boot Sale: on the A52 between Grantham and
Nottingham, NG13 0EE; www.bottesfordgiantcarboot.com
– Sundays and Bank Holiday Mondays, 7 a.m–2 p.m.

London

Battersea

Battersea Boot: Battersea Park School, Battersea Park Road, SW11 5AP; www.batterseaboot.com – Sundays, 12 noon–5 p.m.

Bounds Green

Bounds Green: Bounds Green School, Bounds Green Road, N11 2QG – Sundays from 7 a.m.

Hatton Cross

Hatton: opposite Hatton Cross Underground and bus station, Middlesex TW14 9QP – Sundays, from 7 a.m.

Kilburn

St Mary's Car Boot Sale: St Mary's Church Of England Primary School, Quex Road, NW6 4PG; www.thelondoncarbootco.com – Saturdays, 10 a.m.–3 p.m.

Shepperton

Shepperton Car Boot Sale: New Road, Shepperton, Middlesex TW17 0QQ – Saturdays, 8.30 a.m.

Stoke Newington

Princess May: Princess May School, Barretts Road, N16 8DF; www.thelondoncarbootco.co.uk – Saturdays, 9 a.m.–3 p.m.; Sundays, 9 a.m.–2 p.m.

Wimbledon

Wimbledon Car Boot Sale: Wimbledon Stadium, Plough Lane, SW17 0BL – Wednesdays, 10.30 a.m.–2 p.m.; Saturday & Sunday, 7 a.m.–1.30 p.m.

Manchester, Greater

Sunday Market & Car Boot: New Smithfield Market, Whitworth Street, Openshaw, Manchester M11 2WJ; www.manchester.gov.uk/info/200066/markets – Sundays, 5 a.m.–2 p.m.

Bowlers Car Boot: Bowlers Exhibition Centre, Longbridge Road, Trafford Park, Manchester M17 1SN; www.bowlerscarboot.co.uk – Sundays, 7 a.m.–2 p.m.

Merseyside

Beryl's Booty, The Poulton Vics, Poulton Bridge Road, Wallasey CH44 5SW – Sundays, from 8 a.m.

Car Bootle, behind The Merton pub, Stanley Road/Trinity Road, Bootle L69 9BN; www.carbootle.co.uk – Sundays, from 6 a.m.

Metropolitan Cathedral Car Boot Sale, car park, Mount Pleasant, Liverpool L3 5TQ, www.liverpoolmetrocathedral.org.uk/events – Saturdays, 8 a.m.–12 noon.

Midlands, West

Hockley Heath: Box Trees Farm, Stratford Road, Hockley Heath, Solihull, Birmingham B94 6EA; www.hockleyheathcarboot.com – Sundays, from 6 a.m.

Stafford Car Boot: Stafford Common, Stone Road, Stafford ST16 1NS; www.gocarbootsales.com – Sundays, from 6 a.m.

Col's Car Boot Sale: the field, Himley Bypass B4176 near junction with the A449, WV5 0LU; www.colscarboot.co.uk – Wednesdays, Sundays and Bank Holidays, from 6 a.m.

Furnace End: Laxes Farm, Sandy Lane, Over Whitacre, Furnace End, Warwickshire B46 2NL; www.furnaceendcarboot.co.uk – Sundays and bank Holidays, from 5.30 a.m.

Maypole Car Boot Sale: Dark Lane, Birmingham B47 5BX – from 7 a.m.

Norfolk

Harleston Car Boot Sale: The Apollo Club, Mendham Lane, Harleston IP20 9DN – Sundays, from 10 a.m.

Lazyboots Car Boot Sale: Sprowston Park & Ride, Wroxham Road, Norwich NR7 8RN – Sundays, from 9 a.m.

Northamptonshire

Car Boot & Farmers' Market: Holcot Showground, Poplar Farm, Poplar Lane, Holcot NN6 9SN, www.holcot-showground.co.uk – Saturdays, from 9 a.m.

Potterspury Car Boot: Moorgate Farm, Moorend Road, Potterspury NN12 7QG; www.potterspurycarboot.co.uk – Sundays, from 8 a.m.

Northumberland

Corbridge Car Boot Sale: Tynedale Rugby Club, Corbridge NE45 5AY; www.carbootfair.co.uk – Wednesdays, from 9.30 a.m.

Nottinghamshire

Oldcotes: near Retford S81 8JE – Sundays and Bank Holiday Mondays, 5.30 a.m.–2.30 p.m.

Oxfordshire

Tetsworth: 'The Field', Tetsworth, Oxford OX9 7AT;
www.tetsworthcarboots.co.uk – Sundays, 8 a.m.–1 p.m.

Witney Car Boot Sale: Ducklington Showground, on the A415
Witney to Abingdon road, Witney OX29 7YL
– Sundays and Bank Holidays, from 12 noon.

Shropshire

West Midlands Showground Car Boot Sale: Agricultural
Showground, Berwick Road, Shrewsbury SY1 2PF
– Sundays, from 7 a.m.

Somerset

Massive Nailsea and Wraxhall Car Boot Sale: just off the Bristol
Road, Wraxhall, Nailsea BS48 1JR – Saturdays, from 8 a.m.

Suffolk

Stonham Barns Traditional Car Boot Sale: Stonham Barns,
Pettaugh Road, Stonham Aspal IP14 6AT;
www.fishface.co/stonhambarnscarboot – Sundays, from 8 a.m.

Rougham Airfield Car Boot Sale: Rougham Industrial Estate,
on the A14 Bury St Edmunds-Ipswich Road, IP30 9ND;
www.roughamairfieldsundaymarket.co.uk/carbootsale
– Saturdays and Sundays, from 8.30 a.m.

Surrey

Nuthill: Nuthill Fruit Farm, southbound A3, Ripley, near Guildford
GU23 7LW; www.facebook.com/Nuthillcarbootsale
– Sundays, from 7 a.m.–2 p.m.

Surrey Giant: Priest Hill, Banstead Road, East Ewell KT17 3HH
– Saturdays, from 6 a.m.

Dorking Car Boot Sale: Station Approach, Dorking RH4 1TF
– Sundays, 7 a.m.–1 p.m.

Fairfield Halls: multi-storey car park, Fairfield Halls, Barclay Road,
Croydon CR0 1JN; www.addingtonbootfair.co.uk
– Sundays, from 6.30 a.m.

Sussex, East
Brighton Raceourse: Freshfield Road, Brighton BN2 6XZ;
www.brightoncarbootsale.co.uk – Sundays, 10.30 a.m.–4 p.m.

Mammoth Boot Fair: Cophall and Bramley Farms, on the A22, Polegate,
near Eastbourne BN26 6QN; www.mammothbootfairs.co.uk
– Sundays and Bank Holiday Mondays, from 6 a.m.

Sussex, West
Pease Pottage Car Boot Sale: Hardriding Farm, Pease Pottage,
Crawley RH11 9AA; www.peasepottagecarbootsale.co.uk
– Sundays, 7 a.m.–2 p.m.

Horsham Car Boot Sale: on the A26 near Faygate, Horsham
RH12 4SG; www.horshamcarbootsale.co.uk
– Saturdays, from 7 a.m.

Tyne & Wear
Tranwell Car Boot Sale: on the main Morpeth-Ponteland Road,
NE61 3YJ; www.nobles-promotions.co.uk
– Sundays and Bank Holiday Mondays, from 12 noon.

Seaham Car Boot Sale: on the B1278 Ryhope to Seaham coast road, Sunderland SR7 7AG; www.nobles-promotions.co.uk
– Saturdays, from 12 noon, Sundays and Bank Holidays, from 11 a.m.

Wiltshire
Dauntsey Car Boot Sale: Old Dairy Farm, Dauntsey Lock, Chippenham SN15 4HF; www.dauntseycarboot.co.uk
– Sundays, from 7 a.m.

Worcestershire
Ketch Boot Sale: the Ketch field, Taylors Lane, near the junction of the A38 and A4440 at Carrington Bridge WR5 3HW; www.ketchbootsale.com
– Sundays and bank Holiday Mondays, 6 a.m.–1 p.m.

Arrow Car Boot: Bartleet Rd, Redditch B98 0DQ; www.daredcarboot.co.uk – Sundays, 5.30 a.m.–2 p.m.

Yorkshire
Wetherby Giant Car Boot: The Racecourse, York Road, Wetherby, West Yorkshire LS22 5EJ; www.giantbootfairs.com/wetherby-racecourse-sunday
– Sundays and Bank Holiday Mondays, from 7 a.m.

Otley Car Boot Sale: Wharfedale Farmers' Auction Mart, Otley, Leeds, West Yorkshire LS21 3BD; www.otleycarbootsale.co.uk
– Sundays, 12 noon–4 p.m.

North Cave Sunday Market & Carboot Sale: Newport Road, North Cave, East Riding HU15 2NU; www.northcavemarket.com/about
– 7 a.m.–1 p.m.

East Yorkshire Car Boot Sale: opposite the Golf Course, Danes Dyke, Flamborough, Bempton, Bridlington, East Riding YO13 1AA; www.bpmarkets.co.uk – Sundays, from 8 a.m.

Keepmoat Car Boot Sale: Keepmoat Stadium, Stadium Way, Lakeside, Doncaster DN4 5JW; www.doncaster.gov.uk/sections – Sundays, 6.30 a.m.–12.30 p.m.

Scotland
Aberdeen
Thainstone Sunday Market and Car Boot Sale: Thainstone Centre, Inverurie AB51 5XZ – Sundays, 9 a.m.–4 p.m.

Dundee
Hilltown Market & Car Boot Sale: Main Street, Dundee DD3 7HN; www.hilltownmarket.co.uk – Saturdays and Sundays, from 7.30 a.m.

Edinburgh
Omni Car Boot Sale: Omni Car Park Edinburgh EH1 3AA; www.onlyinedinburgh.com/shopping – Sundays, 9 a.m.–1 p.m.

Glasgow
Polmadie Car Boot Sale: Jessie Street, near Shawfield Stadium, Polmadie G42 0PG; www.polmadiecarbootsale.co.uk – Saturdays and Sundays, 6 p.m.–2.30 p.m.; Wednesdays, 8 a.m.–2 p.m.

Blochairn: 130 Blochairn Road G21 2DU; www.loveyourlocalmarket.org.uk – Sundays, 6.30 a.m.–3 p.m.

Perth
Errol: Errol Airfield, Errol PH2 7TB; www.morrisleslie.com – Sundays, 9 a.m.–3 p.m.

Index